Praise for *Culturally Responsive*

"Marina and Seth's wisdom and stories helped me bett... ...derstand what I've ...... and heard in classrooms around the world, and reflect on how I can be better with kids of every background."

—**Mike Goldstein,** Founder, Match Education, Boston

"Scholars have dissected cultural responsiveness, alerting educators of its importance, but educators are still left with the question of 'how do we actually do this in schools?' The authors extend current knowledge into practical, digestible nuggets of wisdom that concretize and demystify cultural responsiveness for educators."

—**Josephine M. Kim,** Senior Lecturer on Education at Harvard University

"In this engaging and highly readable primer on cross-cultural communications for educators Marina Lee and Seth Leighton offer an original synthesis of knowledge based on scholarship and on practice with practical exercises that can help the reader become more self-aware and competent in navigating cross-cultural exchanges. Their own lived experience, as a multicultural family and as global educators, uniquely qualifies them to speak with authority and authenticity about the potential of true communication that bridges cultures. This book will empower educators to realize the potential that lies in culturally diverse classrooms and schools."

—**Fernando M. Reimers,** Ford Foundation Professor of the Practice of International Education, Harvard Graduate School of Education

Culturally Responsive Conversations

Culturally Responsive Conversations

Connecting with Your Diverse School Community

Marina Minhwa Lee
Seth Leighton

JB JOSSEY-BASS™
A Wiley Brand

Library of Congress Cataloging-in-Publication Data:

Names: Lee, Marina M. (Marina Minhwa), author. | Leighton, Seth, author.
Title: Culturally responsive conversations : connecting with your diverse
  school community / Marina M Lee, Seth Leighton.
Description: Hoboken, New Jersey : Jossey-Bass, [2023] | Includes index.
Identifiers: LCCN 2022059904 (print) | LCCN 2022059905 (ebook) | ISBN
  9781119849155 (paperback) | ISBN 9781119849186 (adobe pdf) | ISBN
  9781119849179 (epub)
Subjects: LCSH: Multicultural education—United States. | Inclusive
  education—United States.
Classification: LCC LC1099.3 .L454 2023 (print) | LCC LC1099.3 (ebook) |
  DDC 370.1170973—dc23/eng/20230113
LC record available at https://lccn.loc.gov/2022059904
LC ebook record available at https://lccn.loc.gov/2022059905

Cover Design: Wiley
Cover Image: © FoxysGraphics/Getty Images
Author Photos: (Lee) Courtesy of Marina Lee, (Leighton) Photo by Justin Knight

SKY10041774_012423

For Madeline Eung Raehui

CONTENTS

ACKNOWLEDGMENTS

Turning an idea into a book was both challenging and rewarding. We especially want to thank the individuals who helped make this happen. We are incredibly grateful for the contributions of research and experiences from students, colleagues, and friends to this book; whether small or large, the friendly spirit and assistance were always significant and meant much more to us than words can express.

Alexandra Koch-Liu

Anthony J. Lee

Amardeep Bhatia

Amelia Stevens

Annie Dong

Aparna Prasad

April J. Remfrey

Ava Shaw

Bernard West

Caroline Min

Chris Zhengda Lu

Christina Linden

Chujie Qiu

Claudia Gonzalez Salinas

David Hawkins

Derek O'Leary

Diana Rangraves

Donovan Richards

Karen V. Wynn, PhD.

Elaine Yining Yan

Fr. Jaehwa Lee

Grace Haddad

Graeme Peele

Hanjing Wang

Hanson Liu

Harry Gallen

James Holden

Jane Namussis

Jean Louis

Jeffrey Li

John Youngho Lee

Joshua Andrew Guo

Julie Moloney

Junming Xing

Kara Madden

Kelly Lu

Linus Law

Metta Dael

Midori Yasamura

Naeun Ruby Koo

Nathaniel Dvorkin

Peter Berzilos

Rebecca Grappo

Rebecca Leighton

Ryan Jin

Sam Fleischmann

Sanaa Gupta

Sanjna Srinivasan

Sarah Loring de Garcia

Shirley Brito

Sonya Pareek

Sophia Tanh

Tammy Alt

Tejas West

Teo Salgado

We are grateful for the guidance of our mentors over the years, including Jerry Murphy, Fernando Reimers, Monica Higgins, Josephine Kim, John Curtis Perry, Juliana Chen, Sung-Yoon Lee, Steven Koltai, Molefi Mataboge, Jed Willard, Michael Goldstein, and countless other colleagues and friends from UNESCO APEID, the Korean Development Institute, Tokyo Parawood, the University of Gondar, Praphamontree School, Harvard Graduate School of Education, the Fletcher School of Law and Diplomacy, and many, many, many schools around the world with whom we've had the good fortune to work.

We express our gratitude to the amazing community of global educators at Envoys, who have taught us both how to truly collaborate across geographic and cultural borders. Special thanks to Felipe Correa, Isabel Eslava, Luis Garcia, Angela Gomez, Daniela Gomez, Annie Harold, Mason Hults, Daniel Matallana, Annie Peuquet, and Laura Rocha for their constant support, advice, and inspiration.

We thank the team at Cogita Education Initiatives, past and present, who have stood strong and compassionate through the years. They are indisputably a group of creative souls who give it their all to educate responsibly. With their intelligence, grace, and humor, they have given a new definition to teamwork, always inspiring me to do and be better as a person and a member of this power team.

Cindy Xuejiao Lin	Jill K. Schaffer	Tingjun (Tina) Liu
Diana Xiunan Jin	Jessie Zhijie Yang	Yingyi (Wenny) Lin
Haoyi (Vivian) Li	Nora Yasamura	

Marina would also like to thank our colleagues and wonderful team members who have supported our important work with families in meaningful ways: Caitlin McGuire, Julie Moloney, Kate Milani, and Tammy Alt.

Thanks to the Jossey-Bass and Wiley team who helped us so much in shepherding us in the creation of our first book. Special thanks to Amy Fandrei, acquisitions editor; Mary Beth Rossworm, editorial assistant; Pete Gaughan, managing editor; Tom Dinse, development editor; Premkumar Narayanan, content refinement specialist; Julie Kerr, copyeditor; and the composition team at Straive for your patience and support.

We thank our nieces and nephews, Alex, Daphne, Emilia, and Magnolia, for their curiosity, bravery, and wit.

Seth would like to thank his parents, Arlene and Jeff, and brother, Max, for modeling how to navigate the world with empathy, understanding, and respect. Marina would like to thank Gomo and Elena and her family of educators, especially her talented siblings, Anthony J. Lee, Sophia Lee Tanh, and Father Jaehwa Lee, and especially her father and dear mother, John and Regina, whose sacrifices and courage have always given strength for the path ahead.

ABOUT THE AUTHORS

Born in Incheon, South Korea, **Marina Minhwa Lee** moved to the United States at a young age, gaining an early perspective on the role of students in serving as cross-cultural "brokers" for families. A former biological researcher, Marina earned her Master of Education from Harvard Graduate School of Education, where her studies focused on immigration, education, and identities.

Marina went on to found Cogita Education Initiatives, a leading provider of educational advising services that empowers students to connect together for the common good. Cogita is committed to enlightening and educating global leaders by cultivating their potential to be changemakers for their generation. Through Cogita, Marina has worked with hundreds of immigrants and international families on transitions to the U.S. educational culture. She is a professional member of the Independent Educational Consultants Association, the National Association of College Admission Counseling, and The Association of Boarding Schools. She consults regularly with leading independent schools on international student support, cultural competency training, and global education curriculum. She can be reached at marinalee@cogitaeducation.com.

Seth Leighton grew up in a small town on the coast of Maine, regularly exploring the outdoors with his friends and family. After attending the local public school in rural Maine, his desire for adventure and exploration has led him around the world, and he has lived, worked, and traveled across North America, South America, Asia, Africa, Europe, and Australia.

Seth co-founded Envoys, a unique organization that partners with innovative teachers and schools to push the boundaries of possibility for global education. Using a blended model of online courses and focused international travel programming, Envoys builds the skill sets associated with global competency. Seth graduated cum laude from Harvard College and has earned advanced degrees from the Harvard Graduate School of Education and the Fletcher School of Law and Diplomacy. Seth can be reached at Seth@envoys.com.

PERSONAL NOTES FROM THE AUTHORS

PERSONAL NOTE FROM MARINA LEE: THIS IS MY WHY

At five years old, I immigrated to the United States of America from Incheon, South Korea.

It was very clear to me, even at that age, that there were certain gender expectations within my family, no matter where I lived. I distinctly recall my parents scolding me for not pouring the water properly into the glasses or setting the dinner plates down delicately. As per their training and patterned behaviors, each time they were prefaced with, "Girls should . . ."

I didn't realize until college that many of the gender expectations from my family and my school community contradicted each other. Each seemed to define what successful members of a community looked like:

- If I followed one set of expectations, I would be considered a disempowered woman.
- If I followed the other, I would be a bold, unrighteous woman brought up without manners, therefore shaming myself and my family.

Even as young as 10 years old, I cut up fruit and made coffee for my father's guests and friends of his or the family who visited our home. I often sat with them for a few minutes and asked about how they were doing, allowed them to ask me questions about school and grades, and then went upstairs to my room to study.

Schoolwork was the only excuse that would be a good enough reason not to stay long with the guests. I excused myself politely, indicating I had a lot of schoolwork to do. I'd get kind nods and enthusiastic "of course, of course" and other words of approval. In retrospect, they were expressions of appreciation for following a culturally conditioned norm everyone could rely on.

Even if a child providing snacks to guests was not expected in some households, it was worthy of praise when she did. *Yejul ee joh tah*, meaning I was brought up with such strong etiquette, reflecting the good family upbringing and being a good girl for following their norm.

Almost any Korean household would agree that my role at the time wasn't surprising to them and would receive a lot of micro-gender-specific admiration. If one of my brothers were to set up fruit for the guests, the praise would have been different, expressing an out-of-the-ordinary surprise and novelty.

FRIENDS OPENED ME TO ANOTHER PERSPECTIVE

When my friends came over and saw me prepare these snacks, they were confused. Most feminists among us, or what we thought of like feminism, said I was a servant to men. They did not understand why I needed to bring my parents' guests anything. There was no praise from them. I felt embarrassed by what they thought of me, whereas I thought I was doing the right thing in my family.

Antithetical to this is how girls are brought up in the United States. Here, being bold, independent, and even fierce is a good thing. Not speaking up means you don't have an opinion of your own, which means you don't think critically or have a strong sense of self, not that you were gracious enough to let others speak their minds and listen to them.

It was not surprising then when my primary school teacher asked my parents to meet her, that although I was top of my class in grades and getting an A, she told them I was too quiet. I needed to speak up in class and share more of my opinions. This was what would jeopardize my grade. My father told me I needed to do better in school. Without realizing the impact of her words, my teacher just made my father speak with me about values that seemed to go against those I was brought up with. I was told conflicting messages, and I didn't know how to reconcile them. This started a spiral of identity questioning that inevitably pitted two parts of my identity against each other, and it felt like there could be only one winner.

WITHIN CULTURAL CLARITY: WHAT IS GOOD AND BAD

What I thought was "good" was "bad" and propagated disempowerment of women in U.S. society. I was a part of a regression seen through the lens of my friends'—and many other—"white" adults' eyes.

As I grew older, I didn't fully understand the complexity of cultural contexts beyond our linear color graph of good, bad, and grey areas. The grey area implied it could be good or bad depending on the context. I have now discovered that culturally influenced behavior, customs, and traditions don't fit into these bipolar, two-dimensional extremes with the grey area in between—that is, there's no possibility of many traditions having the potential to be either good or bad, right or wrong.

I hope this book allows others to see instead that these traditions are, on the whole, linked to another plane of existence that is deeply meaningful to the individual and families. They are tied to the practice and historical connections that have shaped our values and, thus, influenced our identity.

PERSONAL NOTE FROM SETH LEIGHTON

My childhood was characterized by a distinct lack of cultural diversity. Growing up in the 1980s and 1990s in the largely homogenous state of Maine, my interactions with cultures different from my own were limited to the stereotypes portrayed through American entertainment and media at the time.

While my parents, teachers, and greater community, by and large, provided consistent messages for sensitivity and tolerance, like many white Americans, I grew up in a context that supported a sense of my culture being the fundamental "correct" one, and the basis for comparison between all other ways of being. College provided one immediate shake for this perspective, but it was not until I was able to put myself into a wholly new situation that I began to truly appreciate the challenges of living in a cross-cultural milieu.

BROADENING MY WORLD, AND MY WORLDVIEW

My international career began shortly after college when I took a volunteer teaching assignment at a rural high school in the Rayong Province of Thailand. The first few weeks of my time in Rayong were a whirlwind of work at the school, fighting through the normal experiences of any first-time teacher trying desperately to stay ahead with lesson planning and classroom dynamics. I was very lucky to have experienced colleagues to rely on for the basics of student management and to listen to ideas for creative lessons and activities. Very gradually, I built a degree of confidence in my own identity as an educator and took heart in the real progress I saw in my students.

While at the school, I was placed with a host family who owned a large furniture factory. My one-room apartment was perched inside the factory, and my door opened out on 400 people crafting, assembling, and boxing rubberwood furniture for shipment around the world.

While my host family was incredibly generous and amazingly kind, my hometown community seemed far away, and I felt a real disconnect from the people in my immediate surroundings that was hard to manage. Having grown up in a small town in rural Maine, I was accustomed to a sense of neighborliness that was hard to picture occurring in my present circumstances. The physical and cultural distance from those around me seemed impossible to bridge—how would I ever be able to start a conversation?

However, my feeling of connection would come back from the strangest set of circumstances, as one night I got a knock on my door from the brother in my host family. There had been a delay in manufacturing, and an order had to be shipped out immediately. Could I help with the packing?

Feeling a bit awkward, but eager to be of use, I took a spot on the factory floor. I was greeted not with wariness, or even ambivalence, but instead with warm smiles and a happy sense of camaraderie. I was handed a roll of shipping tape and given the task of closing off the box of folding wooden chairs, destined for the shelves of Crate & Barrel.

That experience gave me a true immersion into the Thai concept of *sanuk*. More than having fun, sanuk is about finding a gentle humor and pleasure in any activity. Jokes, songs, and consistent friendly banter were the norm on the assembly and packing lines, and made the hours fly by.

Soon I was on the factory floor on a regular basis. Welcomed in no small part as a teacher of many of their children, I developed a real sense of belonging with the factory workers. My Thai slowly improved, and the reality of this "far end" of the global supply chain became very real for me, forever altering my perception of how products are made and how benefits of employment and trade are distributed around the world. Most importantly, it was quite humbling to feel such openness from people whose backgrounds were so different from mine.

CONTINUING MY JOURNEY

Since my time in Thailand, my experiences interacting with people with views of the world that are radically different from my own have only grown. When I was 26 years old, I received a fellowship from the U.S. Department of State to teach at a university in the city of Gondar in northern Ethiopia.

This was a metropolis of some 250,000 people, with barely a handful of foreigners living full time, mostly involved with the university and medical school. Gondar itself was a former capital of Ethiopia, with the massive fort still standing as a symbol of the Emperor Fasilides's seventeenth-century kingdom that stretched over most of Northern Africa. By the time I arrived, the city (and the country) had suffered through a combination of drought, corruption and misrule, and foreign occupation that had devastated its economy for years. Things were (and are) incredibly difficult for my students. Incredibly bright, talented, and hardworking, they faced daily challenges of supplies and materials, yet they preserved and served as a daily source of motivation for me.

Roughly two months into my time in Ethiopia, I developed a cough and mild fever. What might have kept me home in bed for a morning in another place felt like a major cause for concern in this isolated community, so I headed into the local clinic to see what might be occurring. In a tiny office with chemical reagents housed in recycled plastic milk containers, a lab coat–clad doctor drew my blood for testing. I went over to his office and waited a short while, and finally the doctor came in with the results.

"Your bloodwork has come in and shows signs of malaria. Do you agree? If so, we would like you to start you on antimalarial medication."

I was momentarily dumbfounded—the idea that a medical professional would ask for my "agreement" on a diagnosis was totally outside of my way of thinking. After a moment, I realized this unique phrasing was a small sign of a slightly different framework around decision-making, wherein no important judgments could be made without some sense of discussion and consensus. With this in mind, I agreed with the verdict, and returned to my home for a few admittedly harrowing days of recovery.

I have been amazingly fortunate that my professional life has given me the opportunity to work closely with people from around the world. As the founder of an educational travel organization, I collaborate on a daily basis with people from drastically different sociocultural backgrounds from my own. For this book, I wish to impart some of the frameworks and lessons that I've learned along the way, and, most importantly, to ensure that the kindness I have had in my life continues to be "paid forward" by well-intentioned educators everywhere.

PART I

SETTING THE STAGE

1

IMMIGRATION AND EDUCATION IN THE USA

This chapter provides background on how the goals and means of education have evolved over the history of the United States, moving from the pre-colonial period through the advent of the "common school" and progressive educational movements. We review the ways in which schools have responded to the waves of immigration that created modern America and consider the extent to which the concept of school in the United States both shapes and is shaped by the changing demographics of the student bodies.

This chapter concludes with self-reflective exercises to help educators consider the ways their own experience of school has impacted their views of citizenship, both intentionally and unintentionally. Prompts are given for educators to begin to plan out their learning goals related to developing a sense of "American" identity for students from different cultural backgrounds.

THE GREAT EXPERIMENT

In its most rose-colored and idealistic view, the political institutions of the United States can be regarded as a "great experiment," organizing individuals from a wide variety of social, economic, geographic, and cultural backgrounds under a common value system prioritizing "life, liberty, and the pursuit of happiness." The lofty democratic principles of equal rights, individual freedoms, and government by a majority have continued to be tested as waves of immigration have changed the demographics of the country.

The idea of education as the primary means to meet these tests has been present from the nation's earliest days. Across the New England colonies, each town was established as a religious republic, and "the school everywhere in America arose as a child of the Church"[1] from the onset of the colonial period. Puritan leaders pushed the Massachusetts General Court to issue the "Old Deluder Satan" Act of 1647, making literacy a legal requirement punishable by fine:

> That every Township in this Jurisdiction, after the Lord hath increased them to the number of fifty Housholders, shall then forthwith appoint one within their town to teach all such children as shall resort to him to write and read, whose wages shall be paid either by the Parents or Masters of such children, or by the Inhabitants in general . . .
>
> And it is further ordered, that where any town shall increase to the number of one hundred Families or Housholders, they shall set up a Grammar-School, the Masters thereof being able to instruct youth so far as they may be fitted for the Universitie.[2]

While the responsibility for educating children varied across the colonies between the individual family and the larger community, the post-Revolution mindset saw the need for developing the "common school." Drawing upon Enlightenment ideals, Thomas Jefferson called for the creation of elementary schools across Virginia in his widely noted 1779 Bill for the More General Diffusion of Knowledge, declaring:

> At every of these schools shall be taught reading, writing, and common arithmetic, and the books which shall be used therein for instructing the children to read shall be such as will at the same time make them acquainted with Græcian, Roman, English, and American history. At these schools all the free children, male and female, resident within the respective hundred, shall be intitled to receive tuition gratis, for the term of three years, and as much longer, at their private expence, as their parents, guardians or friends, shall think proper.[3]

In Jefferson's view, these publicly supported and managed schools would provide the citizenry with the basic literacy and numeracy skills seen as necessary for the development of the nation as a whole. Presaging the arguments that would determine first the common school movement of the 1800s and the progressive developments of the 1900s, Jefferson argued that the country as a whole would benefit from public investments in education.

Despite these lofty ideals expressed by Jefferson and other Founding Fathers, the end of the 1700s saw a "patchwork pattern of schools, most of which were conducted under the auspices of private schoolmasters or sectarian religious groups."[4] While upper classes maintained access to higher learning, the ability to gain skills and knowledge necessary for productive work for the masses was largely dependent on apprenticeships or family-based learning, limiting the opportunities for upward mobility. As the century turned, newfound social conditions and a rapidly industrializing nation prompted renewed pressure for a more organized approach to widespread public education.

THE RISE OF THE COMMON SCHOOL

As often in American education, what were widespread societal pressures became personified in one "heroic individual," in this case the educational reformer Horace Mann, often referred to as the Father of the Common School. An active barrister and politician, Mann was elected to the Massachusetts State Senate as a Boston representative in 1835, serving as the Senate President from 1836 to 1837. During his time in the Senate, Mann focused his energies on infrastructure, funding the construction of railroads and canals. In 1837, Mann departed his law practice and legislative position to take on the duties of secretary to the newly established state board of education in Massachusetts. Once he assumed this role, Mann withdrew from all other professional and business engagements, and became wholly dedicated to educational reform.

In 1838, Mann founded *The Common School Journal*, targeting the issues surrounding public education in the United States and promulgating the following six principles:

1. The public should no longer remain ignorant.
2. Education should be paid for, controlled, and sustained by an interested public.
3. Education will be best provided in schools that embrace children from a variety of backgrounds.
4. Education must be nonsectarian.
5. Education must be taught using the tenets of a free society.
6. Education should be provided by well-trained, professional teachers.

Mann led the creation of numerous schools throughout Massachusetts, serving families from a wide range of socioeconomic backgrounds in both urban and rural areas. Drawing on his legislative experience, Mann drove the creation of tax-supported elementary public education in several states, along with the professionalization (and, as a continued trend, feminization) of the teaching force.

Mann's vision for institutionalizing teacher training took place mainly through the development of "normal schools" setting standards for pedagogical and curricular norms. In 1839, the first of these state-funded schools was established in Lexington, Massachusetts, maintaining continuous operations and eventually becoming Framingham State University. Normal schools were open to women, providing new opportunities for women to enter the workforce.

Mann's success in bringing about common schools came from his strong and repeated arguments that universal education was an essential precursor for a stable and harmonious polis. This message resonated across the growing class of new property owners, especially only a few generations removed from the American Revolution. Mann's assertion that the sanctity of "life, liberty, and the pursuit of happiness" was dependent on a highly literate and numerate population held both a practical as well as a patriotic appeal. As the historian Ellwood P. Cubberley noted:

> No one did more than [Mann] to establish in the minds of the American people the conception that education should be universal, non-sectarian, free, and that its aims should be social efficiency, civic virtue, and character, rather than mere learning or the advancement of sectarian ends.[5]

Mann's efforts catalyzed universal public education in the Northern United States during the 1800s, with continued attention toward the standardization of structured curriculum and away from the "single schoolmarm" model of the traditional colonial communities. By 1864, all students in the city of Chicago were divided into age-based grades, with each grade following a distinct course of study for each subject.[6]

INDUSTRIALIZATION AND SCHOOLING

While the common school movement began to influence the educational systems of the Southern states, the structural realities of slave-based economies made the establishment of free public schools untenable until after the Civil War. As the Reconstruction era took hold, the developmental needs of the South and concurrent reorganization of civil society created the space for the common school to become a reality across the newly re-formed nation. Robert E. Lee expressed the needs of the South in a private letter as:

> So greatly have those interests [educational] been disturbed in the South, and so much does its future condition depend upon the rising generation, that I consider the proper education of its youth one of the most important objects now to be attained, and one from which the greatest benefits may be expected. Nothing will compensate us for the depression of the standard of our moral and intellectual culture, and each State should take the most energetic measures to revive the schools and colleges, and, if possible, to increase the facilities for instruction and to elevate the standard of learning.[7]

By the advent of the twentieth century, the Southern states had experienced "the greatest educational awakening in their history,"[8] with new educational legislation setting out minimum requirements and subjects of instruction. Within the span of one century, education in every state in the nation had transitioned from mainly religious oversight, mixed in with familial instruction and both formal and informal apprenticeships, to a wholly secular undertaking funded by the public at large, with set curriculum, professional instructors, and requirements for progression.

As the rapidly industrializing nation saw continued societal and economic changes, the nature of debates around the purpose of education in the United States evolved as well. Public awareness of the changes in American society was driven in part by the developments in communication networks that created new connections throughout the growing nation. Between 1870 and 1880, the number of newspapers in America doubled, demonstrating both the growing demand for knowledge of current events and the growing supply of educated journalists and reporters. Readership in other mediums grew apace, with the circulation of weekly magazines exceeding that of newspapers in the 1890s. This widespread appetite for reading was evidenced by the astounding *Ladies Home Journal* reaching over 700,000 copies in 1892,[9] reaching more than 1% of the nation's population.

The rapid onset of news and information flows came hand-in-hand with the advance of railroads as a means of reliable and inexpensive transportation. Miles of rail in operation grew from 35,085 in 1865 to 190,833 in 1899,[10] connecting both major cities and rural areas alike. As the historian Robert Wiebe pointed out:

> The primary significance of America's new railroad complex lay not in the dramatic connections between New York and San Francisco but in the access a Kewanee, Illinois, or an Aberdeen, South Dakota, enjoyed to the rest of the nation, and the nation to it.[11]

IMMIGRATION AND DEMOGRAPHIC CHANGE

American society transformed from relatively self-contained and self-sufficient rural communities to largely industrialized urban centers. As the population connected and urbanized, it also grew in size and diversity. Vast numbers of immigrants, mostly from Europe, crossed the Atlantic to settle in metropolitan centers seeking to work hard, make money, and begin a new life in the United States. Between 1860 and 1890, 13.5 million new immigrants arrived in the United States.[12] By 1890, the foreign-born population of New York City was approximately 639,943 out of the entire population of 1,515,301,[13] a percentage that mirrors that of the five boroughs in the twenty-first century.

These increases in immigration built on the solid foundations laid with the common schools to begin a massive influx of students into the U.S. secondary school system. From 1850 to 1900, roughly half of 5- to 19-year-olds enrolled in school (at any level). Rates for males and females were similar throughout the period, though rates for blacks were substantially lower than for whites. From 1900 to 1940, however, the overall enrollment rates for 5- to 19-year-olds rose from 51% to 75%, with differences in the white and black enrollment rates shrinking from 23 points in 1900 to 7 points in 1940.[14] The growth of the American common school in latter half of the 1800s created a population who saw the benefits for continued education for their children. As an ever-increasing segment of the population clustered into cities, attendance in secondary schools became both more convenient and more economically beneficial.

As the nation's demographics shifted from rural to urban and continued to diversify from immigration, schools transformed from the representation of a distinct community into a means of mediation between the family unit and the complex society. The focal points of the debate around schooling began to shift from the talents of the individual teacher to the knowledge, skills, and values put forth by the curriculum. In 1893, the National Education Association proposed a curriculum for secondary school students with both college preparation as well as training for modern employment and the new society. This focus on curricular revision and standardization to meet both present and future needs both drove and was driven by America's rapidly modernizing economy and sense of assurance as a global power.

EDUCATIONAL REFORM IN THE TWENTIETH CENTURY: A PERPETUALLY (RE)CREATED NATION

By the time the twentieth century arrived, the course of the new American curriculum was set to be determined by an ongoing debate between traditionalists and reformers. The classical approach drew on centuries of tradition, tied to the Enlightenment ideals around the power of reason and (primarily) European cultural heritage. This group held power through their position in the faculty and administration of esteemed tertiary institutions, and thus held a powerful influence in the academic world. These traditionalists sought to uphold the Protestant traditions and egalitarian values of the colonial and Revolutionary periods in the face of the expanding reach of schools and rapidly changing society. The traditionalist references to the spirit of the Founding Fathers and Constitution continued to influence American curriculum (and politics) throughout the century.

The reformers, meanwhile, could be delineated into three broad groups,[15] each representing a different conception of the content and purpose of the curriculum. The humanist reformers drew on romantic notions of childhood development and the creation of a curriculum that would exist in harmony with student's needs, learning styles, and interests. This movement gained more authority with the demonstrated success at primary levels of Maria Montessori's Casa dei Bambini in the early 1900s. The young children attending Montessori's schools engaged spontaneously with learning materials and showed proficiency in reading and writing far beyond expectations,[16] attracting the interest of prominent educators and making a case for similar approaches for secondary education. For American humanists, the curriculum could become the primary avenue to unleash the natural tendencies within the child for learning.

A less romantic, but compelling, push for reform arose from the sense of the nation as a burgeoning economic powerhouse, with scientific and technological innovation being realized in a wide range of industries. The efficiencies and standardized techniques epitomized by the widely publicized production line of the Ford Motor Company brought about a sense of possibility to eliminate waste and create a socially efficient and effective means of educating the masses. This movement was catalyzed by the hugely influential David Snedden, who served as the first Massachusetts Commissioner of Education from 1909 to 1916 and later a professor of educational sociology at Columbia Teachers College.

Speaking directly against the traditional Classical education, Snedden urged for the development of a scientific-based curriculum to prepare students for the industrial economy, both in the present and the future. In 1922, he published the foundational *Educational Sociology*, which supplied detailed lists of abilities, attitudes, habits, and forms of knowledge to help students advance in the highly competitive world. Snedden championed the idea that every subject, be it Latin, Greek, history, or mathematics, had to be socially useful, as well as the less palatable notion that efficient society should be divided into leaders and followers, with each group trained for a specific role and function.[17] This coldly efficient view of education was based on a vision of a future of work that would require massively diverse specialization of skills, and saw a highly regimented and scientifically based curriculum as the main means for the continued realization of the "American Century."

Standing in opposition to this industrialized view of education were the third set of reformers, those who saw education as the main, if not only, means for fomenting social change. From Lester Frank Ward to John Dewey (and, globally, Paulo Freire), these "philosopher kings" stood as the forerunners of the modern social justice movements that continue to force the nation to come to terms with its past and present. These reformers called for curriculum to be designed to actively shape students to cure societal ills, from political corruption to the ever-present inequalities of race and gender.

After beginning his career as a primary and secondary teacher, Dewey came to promi-nence as a faculty member at the University of Chicago and Columbia University, publish-ing a series of books between 1897 and 1938 that established him as the leading voice for progressive education and liberalism. Dewey took a harsh view of the diversified vocational training as "an instrument of perpetuating unchanged the existing industrial order of soci-ety, instead of operating as a means its transformation," advising instead that curriculum must be designed with the "intention of improving the life we live in common so that the future shall be better than past."[18]

Dewey's inspired calls put the power (and onus) on schools as the primary means to create a new and better nation. Ultimately, the changing conditions of education in America would not be wholly decided by the Progressive calls for social justice, the traditionalist Classical curriculum, the Montessorian fixation on the needs of the child, or the Industrial vision of an efficient ordering of students into set roles. Instead, the American curriculum (writ large) from the twentieth century into modern times has been the result of a loose combination of these four views, put into practice on an ever-evolving population.

The ever-shifting nature of the national debate around the central functions of school in society, around what knowledge is worth knowing and what skills should be imparted to the masses, mirrors the unique nature of the United States as a created nation. As the oft-quoted Oscar Handlin wrote in 1952, "Once I thought to write a history of the immigrants in America. Then I discovered that the immigrants *were* American history."[19]

Indeed, with Native Americans and Alaska Natives constituting less than 3% of the American population in 2020, there are upwards of 320 million Americans who are either immigrants themselves or are a direct descendant of immigrants. In the posthumously pub-lished *A Nation of Immigrants,* John F. Kennedy noted that:

> This was the secret of America: a nation of people with the fresh memory of old traditions who dared to explore new frontiers, people eager to build lives for themselves in a spacious society that did not restrict their freedom of choice and action.[20]

This rosy view, of course, glosses over the abhorrent history of slavery in the United States. In the recorded history of slave trade to the New World, between 1525 and 1866, 12.5 million Africans were shipped to the New World.[21] The vast majority of those who survived disembarked at sugar plantations in the Caribbean and South America, with roughly 600,000 ending up in the United States. The official end of the trans-Atlantic slave trade came with the Act Prohibiting Importation of Slaves, passed in 1800 and taking effect in 1808, creating a dramatic fall in the importation, though not the practice, of slavery. The domestic trade, meanwhile, continued into the 1860s, displacing approximately 1.2 million men, women, and children, the vast majority of whom were born in America.[22]

From the 1820s onwards, immigration to the United States has come in waves, with the European influx cresting in the early 1900s and then falling off rapidly in the post-Depression period. While the Second World War and its immediate aftermath led to a momentary falloff, immigration accelerated again from the 1950s to the present day, with increasingly large proportions coming from Asia and Latin America. These millions of people represent the largest continued migration in world history.

While world events can be seen as having a large influence on the location of departure, the "push" motives for immigrating have generally fallen into three domains:[23] seeking freedom from religious persecution, seeking freedom from political oppression, and seeking better economic opportunities. As well as the ebbs and flows in the pull factors of national sentiment and public policy regarding immigrants.

Indeed, a regularly occurring claim throughout U.S. history has pushed the position that expansive immigration policies have reached the end of their utility, as the population of a new and unsettled country reached its saturation point. The counterpoint, and predominantly "American" sentiment, may have been best expressed by Thomas Jefferson's question:

> Shall we refuse to the unhappy fugitives from distress that hospitality which the savages of the wilderness extended to our fathers arriving in this land? Shall oppressed humanity find no asylum on this globe?[24]

SUMMARY

This chapter provided an introductory review of the initial formations of models for school within the United States. We reviewed the evolution of competing philosophies for the purpose and methods for education, including Progressive calls for social reforms, more traditional Classical curriculum, a Montessori focus on the needs of the child, and technocratic training for industrial purposes. The chapter noted the consistent protests arising with each wave of new arrivals to the United States, despite the longstanding character of the country as a nation of immigrants.

SELF-PRACTICE EXERCISES FOR EDUCATORS

- Consider your own experience as a student in middle and high school. Think about both what was explicitly taught and implicitly conveyed. The set of questions could also be used for a workshop for parents to better relate to their children and for the school to better understand their community members.

- What did you learn about your country's national "character" and ideals?
- What did you learn about how a classroom "should" be run? What were acceptable behaviors for students and teachers? What were the "boundaries" between teachers, students, and parents?
- Who were your classmates? Your teachers? How did their identities and behaviors influence your view of the world? How did you influence theirs?

- Think about your current curriculum and lesson plans. Consider the degree to which each of the following pedagogical philosophies is present in your own teaching practice:
  - Progressivism and social change.
  - Traditional Classical curriculum.
  - The needs of the child.
  - Training for career and job functions.

- Think about what you believe about the rights, responsibilities, and restrictions around life in the United States. What do you wish to impart to your students?

NOTES

1. Cubberley, E.P. (1919). *Public Education in the United States*. Boston: Houghton Mifflin Company, p. 44.
2. The Laws and Liberties of Massachusetts. (1929). Reprinted from the Copy of the 1648 Edition in the Henry E. Huntington Library, with an introduction by Max Farrand. Cambridge, MA: Harvard University Press.
3. Jefferson, T. (1779). A Bill for the More General Diffusion of Knowledge. Founders Online. https://founders.archives.gov/documents/Jefferson/01-02-02-0132-0004-0079.
4. StateUniversity.com Education Encyclopedia. (n.d.). Common school movement: Colonial and Republican schooling, changes in the antebellum era, the rise of the common school. https://education.stateuniversity.com/pages/1871/Common-School-Movement.html#ixzz7FiOy7HdD.
5. Cubberley, E.P. (1919). *Public Education in the United States*. Boston: Houghton Mifflin Company, p. 167.
6. Tyack, D. (1974). *The One Best System: A History of American Urban Education*. Cambridge, MA: Harvard University Press, p. 46.
7. Education in the South: Abstracts of Papers Read at the Sixteenth Conference for Education in the South. (1913). Sixteenth Conference for Education in the South, Richmond, Virginia (15 to 18 April 1913). Issues 21-30, p. 23.
8. Cubberley, E.P. (1919). *Public Education in the United States*. Boston: Houghton Mifflin Company, p. 361.
9. Kliebard, H. (2004). *The Struggle for the American Curriculum 1893-1958, Third Edition*. New York: Routledge Falmer, pp. 2–3.
10. Statistical Abstract of The United States 1900. (1901). Washington D.C.: Bureau of Statistics / Government Printing Office. https://www.census.gov/library/publications/1901/compendia/statab/23ed.html.
11. Wiebe, R.H. (1967). *The Search for Order: 1877-1920*. New York: Farrar, Straus & Giroux, p. 47.

12. Fass, P. (1989). *Outside in: Minorities and the Transformation of American Education*. New York: Oxford University Press.

13. Zervas, T.G. (2017). Finding a balance in education: immigration, diversity, and schooling in urban America, 1880-1900. *Athens Journal of Education* 4 (1): pp. 77–84.

14. National Center for Education Statistics. (1993). 120 Years of American Education: A Statistical Portrait.

15. Kliebard, H. (2004). *The Struggle for the American Curriculum 1893–1958, Third Edition*. Oxfordshire, England: Routledge.

16. Kramer, R. (1976). *Maria Montessori*. Chicago: University of Chicago Press.

17. Drost, W. (1967). *David Snedden and Education for Social Efficiency*. Madison: University of Wisconsin Press.

18. Dewey, J. (1916). *Democracy and Education*. New York: The Macmillan Company, pp. 226, 316.

19. Handlin, O. (1952). *The Uprooted (The epic story of the great migrations that made the American people)*. New York: Grosset & Dunlap.

20. Kennedy, J.F. (1964). *A Nation of Immigrants*. New York: Harper & Row, p. 3.

21. Trans-Atlantic Slave Trade – Database. (n.d.). Slave Voyages. https://www.slavevoyages.org/voyage/database (accessed 22 September 2022).

22. Strochlic, N. (2019). How slavery flourished in the United States. *National Geographic* (23 August).

23. Johnston Area Heritage Association. (2013). US immigration by region and decade: 1821–2000. https://www.jaha.org/edu/discovery_center/push-pull/pdf/immigration_timeline.pdf (aceessed 15 August 2021).

24. Jefferson, T. (1801). First Annual Message to Congress (8 December).

2

IT TAKES MORE THAN
A VILLAGE

This chapter considers the multiple stakeholders with an investment in the positive education of children. Each community has its own set of stakeholder groups with a vested interest in supporting the students in their local schools. Educators must consider which groups exist in their community, and how longstanding power dynamics may impact cross-cultural families, both positively and negatively.

MULTIPLE CULTURAL MODELS

The proverb "it takes a village to raise a child" has become so widely used to become the epitome of a cliché. Prominently used by Hillary Clinton as the title of her 2012 book about transforming society to enable children to become caring adults, this proverb addresses the aspect of children requiring a parental figure for their growth. For a child to grow with the best values and morals, a community must be present in their life to guide them. The rationale behind the proverb is that a community shapes the child's morals, accountability, and sense of life's responsibility and purpose. In some cultures, a child is viewed as a gift from God; therefore, the group's obligation is to rear that child.

The proverb is thought to have African roots. In Kijita (Wajita), there is a proverb that says *Omwana ni wa bhone*, meaning regardless of the biological parent(s) of the child, upbringing belongs to the community.

In Kiswahili, another term for Swahili, the proverb *Mkono moja haulei mwana* directly translates to "One hand does not raise a child" and parallels the same thought.

In Lunyoro (Banyoro), the proverb *Omwana takulila nju emoi* translates to "A child does not grow up only in a single home."

In Kihaya (Bahaya), there is a saying, *Omwana taba womoi*, which translates as "A child belongs not to one parent or home."[1]

We could continue sharing examples from different cultures that confirm the importance of community in a toddler's life. Within the Igbo and Yoruba tribes of Nigeria, children traditionally belonged to the community, and anyone within the community had the right to punish a child. The children also would go through different apprenticeship classes to learn different skills to give back to the community.

COMMUNITY AND STAKEHOLDERS IMPLICATIONS

The societal environment in which a child develops impacts their progress and perceptions, in one way or the other, from childbirth to adulthood. It is a collective responsibility to ensure the child is well taken care of and brings together the teachers, who spend most of their time at school.

This society also includes extended family members, aunts, uncles, grandparents, cousins, neighbors, godparents, friends, counselors, life coaches, and mentors. It is a collective responsibility to raise empathic, courageous, and able children. The objective does not account for what is best for the children but what is best for society.

Each community comprises stakeholder groups invested in seeing the students in their local schools succeed. Time and attention to understanding these groups are critically important for educators and administrators alike. In the United States, school counselors help students solve their interpersonal problems and support growth by ensuring they are self-aware and in touch with themselves. Teachers, meanwhile, have the responsibility to equip the students with information and skills, taking the time to learn each child they interact with to know how best to support them. They are also responsible for ensuring the child can learn independently.

WHO IS IN YOUR VILLAGES?

One of this book's authors (Seth) grew up in Maine. He faced a daily conundrum surrounding getting home from elementary school. When he was 12 years old, two distinct options emerged. The first was the "tried-and-true" school bus. It was a good option for getting to school, as his was close to the last stop in the morning, providing several additional precious minutes of sleep before the quick ride in.

However, due to the forced consistency of roads and schedules, he was also the last stop in the afternoon. This made the ride home nearly two hours of bouncing along the road with an ever-decreasing number of friends and classmates, until finally arriving home in the early evening.

The second option was to take the bus in the morning, and in the afternoon, to ask the driver, a kind gentleman called "Moose" (this was Maine, after all), to drop him off at an early junction for a one-mile walk along the road. The option was, of course, not approved (or known) by his parents, but this was a simpler time, and with two working and trusting parents, he was free to walk with no one the wiser. Of course, this was a moot point during the depth of Maine winters.

During cold winter mornings, he would wait outside, with rapidly freezing hair reminding him of the importance of drying after a shower, until the bus finally pulled up for the short ride to school. In the afternoon, he would gladly sit on the long ride.

Once the snow melted and the sun came out, the decision tree looked entirely different. He would get off the bus, assuring Moose that all was approved, and walk merrily home, reaching his house a solid 60 minutes (or two *Simpsons* episodes) before the bus passed by.

While walking home one day, a pickup truck heading in the opposite direction slowed down, turned around, and then pulled over. A flannel-clad, bearded fella (again, this is Maine) peered down from the cab. He was the father of a friend of his brother.

He smiled kindly and asked, "You are not skipping school, are you?" while offering a lift home. On the short ride, they chatted about the recent spring weather (good), the prospects for the school's basketball team (decent), and the likelihood of a tourist-free summer (poor). As they passed a construction site, the older Mainer commented on the planned building of new cell phone towers as a sign of things changing for the worse, being both a blight on the scenery as well as yet another concession to those "from away." After dropping Seth off at home, the bearded gentleman turned around again and set back off down the road.

Looking back, the concern shown by this Mainer demonstrates five things about the needs of this young stakeholder regarding the role of community in his growth.

Place

From Seth's experience, we can see the community is responsible for ensuring the child is at the right place. The older Mainer inquired about the young Mainer missing school and took it up as his responsibility to ensure he got home before going ahead with his business. He took it upon himself as a friend to the family to ensure the boy got home safe. For this particular Mainer, stopping and turning around was his way of demonstrating and upholding his place in society.

Time

There is a clear need to spend time with and for this young Mainer. He felt it took him longer to get home and decided to be dropped off at an earlier junction. The parents were unaware and did not notice the inconsistency in the arrival time of their son from school during the different seasons. Yet, this difference built early critical-thinking decision-making skills in the youngster. The young Mainer also takes advantage of the fact that his parents trust him and uses it to his advantage. A parent's role is crucial in raising a child. Youngsters need a parental figure who is invested, involved in shaping outlooks and values.

Method

The method of acquiring information comes in many forms. Here we see the older Mainer—Moose—school, bus schedules, and the environment providing him information. Primarily his own senses and looking at the rewarding outcome led to a series of long-term decisions.

This demonstrates adaptation, resourcefulness, and the learned ability to pivot within the critical-thinking framework. Human society is dependent on a school training system for skills, education, community, peer groups, and values. Teachers, mentors, and, in the case of home schooling, parents are the grounding elements toward supporting the creation of a whole individual.

Content

Children should be generally knowledgeable about what is happening in the local community. The definition of the boundaries of this community, and thus the areas of knowledge, is implicit. The expectations are that anyone living in the town past a certain age would know at least the rudiments of behavior, knowledge, and social structures. We would say that the teachers excel in this role. It falls to them to ensure students are equipped with knowledge and basic skills as they advance.

Values

We look to children to always uphold the values of truthfulness. Our future depends on not giving them a window for lies. The community, peer group sets the tone and voice of perceptions. Knowing who is in your village and the trending thoughts, behaviors, and actions confirms that "It takes a village to raise a child."

Here we see this when the older Mainer asks the younger if he skipped school and does not wait for an answer. He decides to drop him home. Younger Mainer also takes advantage of this and requests a drop off earlier. He knows Moose expects the truth and will not think he might be lying about his parents' knowledge.

Children uphold a value around preserving the current status of the town. This is with a concurrent negative view of outsiders and suspicion of progress. It was expected that the cell phone towers and tourists would be perceived with disdain by anyone in the community. This was regardless of their impact on the local economy. Agreement on this point was assumed, not a matter of debate.

Rising Cultural Complexity

When you compare the current society in which we live with the experience shared in the previous section, there are progressive similarities and vast magnitudes. Modernization has brought new dimensions to raising children, and the "village" has as its intimate neighbors online communities and people around the world touching the lives of children. That said, the integral nature of school and educators for a child's development has not changed.

The expansion of urban life and continued immigration and an increase in international students and families have brought a welcome diversity of cultures in schools. Concurrent with this diversity, educators face challenges in providing an equal platform for all the children to learn and supporting students to develop their perspective and take action on issues that matter for our shared future, including social justice and climate change.

This is a highly tendentious and highly important charge for educators, requiring a balancing act between personal viewpoints and those of families and students themselves. For example, a Filipino family with whom Marina worked closely unfortunately experienced severe racism when they first moved to the United States, with the eldest brother regularly harassed by his fellow students, many of whom came from White and Latin American families. This harassment resulted in the development of a spirit of antagonism, especially toward Whites and Latin Americans, from the student, which translated into poor friendships, academics, and behavior at school. The student clashed with his teachers by expressing a viewpoint that "all Latinos are lazy thieves," a perspective unfortunately echoed by his parents.

The solution came from a slow process of establishing a new "village" of educators and community members, including the intervention of trained counselors and educators who were more familiar with discussing bullying within the Filipino cultural context. Instructors adopting inclusivity, where they acknowledge cultural differences and make the children and parents understand that life is still okay, accelerate the child's morals, accountability, and sense of life's responsibility and purpose. Failing to broach topics with a sensitive cultural hand may reinforce a message of hate inadvertently.

For a village to truly provide the full support a child needs, it is usually up to the people in the child's home to be the main caretaker. However, educators need to be mindful of gaps created in the immigrant experience. In another incident with racism for a student from the Dominican Republic, the child responded by negating everything culturally and racially related to her. She became more distant with her own family. As time progressed, the student couldn't speak Spanish well anymore, creating a language barrier with her parents and grandparents. Because of this inability to communicate, the student was unable to feel as connected with her family, making her feel more isolated. If parents are not echoing or don't know how to emphasize the same messages of tolerance that the school is giving out, the child will feel confused. When the situation creates a dearth of parental support, other members of the village must fill in the gaps.

SUMMARY

It takes more than a village to raise a child. Children need guidance from their parents, friends, family, and teachers, all of whom impact their lives. For some families, their cultural norms may have as a part of the village extended family members as well as close friends or familiar educators (tutors, consultants, former teachers, etc.)—some of whom you may hear are called or referred to as "aunties." Additional "villagers" could be members of the student's global community as well as culturally aware specialists either invited in or accessed online.

Schoolwork and assignments involve not only giving and receiving information but also life skills, for example, a teacher ensuring the child cultivates communication. All need an understanding and self-awareness of the child to facilitate full potential. The role of the society could involve neighbors, churches, sporting events, and social avenues to support the child and serve as good examples. We learn by mirroring, and as a member of the metaphorical village, we can exemplify skills we want the children to have. For instance, if parents make a special halal meal for their son's Muslim friend coming to his son's birthday party, they may provide the child direction on how to be respectful and thoughtful of another's religious choices. They would be echoing a communication of respect that he would be learning at school. Understanding that different cultures would have different members in the village and with each member having unique influences in each village would be helpful information to have to communicate effectively with the families. For example, in many more traditional households, the mother is the one managing the student's education. However, the grandparents, as is often common in Russian cultures, would be a powerful participant.

INTERACTIVE SELF-PRACTICE EXERCISES

1. Modernization has impacted the traditional ways in which a child is raised. In your society, you can choose people you consider being part of your village. Examples include

people in your villages such as mentors, life coaches, grandparents, teachers, and nuclear and extended family.

(a) For each person, list three things they taught you, either by example or lessons learned.

(b) Why was this important? How do you and your community benefit? How has this shaped your values or perspective in life?

2. All children should receive support from the community for a better society in the future. A child without a community may be less connected and have fewer social interactions. For a person to survive in a community, they need to learn the basics of interactions by having an opportunity to interact with people. A well-raised individual tends to benefit the community, as they are the future leader of the community.

(a) Describe an instance where you felt disconnected. What was/were the reason(s)? How did this disconnectedness make you feel? What did you do about it?

(b) Describe where an individual within the community helped develop your leadership skills.

3. Address this scenario: You have a family with two children, and it is now time for you to look for a house to buy. You have a checklist on the type of house: the area, details of the house, and other factors. You come across two houses that tick the boxes on what you are looking for. One of the houses with everything you wanted is in a busy neighborhood. As you talk with the realtor, they inform you a gang member was shot the other day around the block. At the other house, although it is smaller than the first, you meet friendly neighbors. Bearing in mind that you have children, you will look for neighborhoods that feel safe. One that gives your children a homey feel where you have neighbors you can trust. You pick the latter. Once you move into the area, there are high chances your child will be invited to birthday parties and soccer camps. You want your child to interact with people from whom they can learn.

(a) Do you think you will choose who is in your village subconsciously as you select a house?

(b) What other elements can you look at to determine if this is the village for your family?

4. You notice that one of your students is withdrawn and does not want to participate in any discussions. She was once very vocal, but all that had changed. As their teacher, you would like to know what is happening and call her to your office. After providing a safe space, you ask her if there is an issue. She tells you that during an in-class small group discussion one of the students told her that she is too dark. A boy proceeded to ask if it

was because she used to live in Africa in the forest with lions. She claims that her classmate said his parents had told her about people who have moved from Africa to the United States. All the students laughed about it, and they called her a bush girl.

(a) What would you say to her, if anything? How would you handle that cultural diversity complexity?

(b) Bearing in mind that the boy heard this from his parents, how can you ensure this does not come off as disrespectful to the boy's family?

(c) Would you bring this up the parents of the girl? If so, how?

EFFECTIVE CONVERSATIONAL POINTS

With a colleague, discuss the following:

- Were there skills you learned from people who were not part of your family? Do you apply any of these skills in your day-to-day or have you applied them anywhere in life?

- Looking back now, do you feel society played a part in your upbringing? Do you feel the role of society in upbringing has changed in recent years? Discuss and share.

- During the pandemic, how did you handle human contact? Did you reach out to a neighbor with whom you never had any conversations earlier? Do you feel like the Covid-19 pandemic has taught us to appreciate our communities more? What has the pandemic taught you on the importance of community? Discuss and share.

NOTE

1. Goldberg, J. (2016). It takes a village to determine the origins of an African proverb. Goats and Soda (30 July). https://www.npr.org/sections/goatsandsoda/2016/07/30/487925796/it-takes-a-village-to-determine-the-origins-of-an-african-proverb.

3

THE INTERPLAY BETWEEN LANGUAGE AND CULTURE

This chapter provides an overview of how differences in patterns of expressed language can arise due to differences in cultural thought patterns. Contrary to common perception, understanding speakers of different languages is not simply a matter of needing "a better bilingual dictionary." Rather, it requires an understanding of how our underlying value systems, lived experiences, and perceptions of the world can interpret the direct and implied messages being conveyed.

We begin with a brief background on how human language has evolved in different ways in different parts of the world, including illustrative examples of variances in meaning both between and within languages. We then examine research on the distribution of values among cultural geographies in the world, noting findings that link the socioeconomic development of a country with different value orientations, and providing some cautions around our innate tendency for social classification. This chapter concludes with practical advice and strategies for educators for language use that helps strike the fine balance of respecting cultural differences while avoiding stereotyping.

EVOLUTION OF VARIATIONS IN LANGUAGE

The relative complexity of human language has evolved in divergent phases over history. This has been influenced by various factors, including the surrounding environment and societal hierarchies within different cultures.

Perhaps the most widely known example of environment impacting language is the oft-cited note of the multiplicity of words for different types of snow used by the Inuit people. The 1911 publication of *Handbook of American Indian Languages*[1] first popularized this environmentally based complexity, making note of the differences between *piegnartoq*, for snow that is solid enough to drive a sled, and *aqilokoq*, for snow that falls without a sound.

Equally as impactful as environment factors have been societal patterns of organization. During the Ayutthua period of Thailand in the fourteenth century, the honorific vocabulary known as *raja-sap* emerged as a way for commoners to talk to and about the royal family. This new category of honorifics broadened over time with different subdialects used for monks, family members, and varying levels of politeness.

Aside from the intrinsic interest, these examples illustrate the tremendous level of difference between the structure of languages. The linguistic relativity theory, often called the Sapir–Whorf hypothesis,[2] suggests that these differences in linguistic structure impact on how people think and see the world and, therefore, our worldviews are inherently dependent on the languages that we speak.

ONE WORD, MANY MEANINGS

The flip side of this reality, of course, means that learning a new language requires understanding how language develops. For effective communication, this includes understanding basic human psychology, the topic's context, as well as the symbols and word markers embedded within a particular dialect.

Given the complexity of language evolution, and the inherent social nature of human life, different meanings can be associated with a single word. A word may have one or more meanings in a native language and another meaning in a second language. In fact, many words have the same spellings and pronunciation but have different meanings and connotations across multiple languages. The similarity in spelling and pronunciation can be because the words come from the same language family or are loan words.

The phenomenon of different languages having different meanings for the same word is known as "false friends." Examples of false friends include:

- "To use the voice" means saying something "aloud" in English, but the same words mean "ancient" in Dutch.

- "Mama" is generally used for mother, but the term means "father" in Georgian.
- "Si" means "yes" in Spanish, but it means "no" in Swahili, and "La" is used for "no" in Arabic.
- "No" is yes in Czech—a short version of "ano."
- "Angel" in English means divine power, but it means "fishing rod" in German and "sting" in Dutch.

False friends are also present in dialects of the same language, as "chips" or "rocket" in the United Kingdom refers to "French fries" and "arugula," respectively, in the United States.

Words can also differ across regions of the same country, as many in the United States may know "pop" in parts of the West, Midwest, and the Pacific Northwest refers to a "soda" primarily along the coasts or "coke" along the South.

ONE WORD, DIFFERENT MEANINGS IN ONE LANGUAGE

One word with more than two meanings is known as a homonym in English. A way to recognize homonyms is by paying attention to the context in which they are being used.

Here are some examples of homonyms.

- "Pen" means a writing instrument as well as a holding area for animals.
- "Book" means a set of papers to read as well as an act of reservation.
- "Tender" can mean sensitive, easily chewed, money, currency, or even refer to chicken strips.
- "Mine" as a noun means a place underground from where minerals are extracted, whereas as a possessive pronoun, it shows one's possession.
- "Interest" as a noun means wanting to learn or know more, and also additional money charged on a borrowed sum or earned on a bank account. As a verb, it means evoking curiosity or grabbing attention.

We recognize that most educators using this book will be holding conversations with families and students using English. Given its prominence in the worlds of commerce, science, and academia, English is unsurprisingly one of the most widely spoken languages globally. The language journal *Ethnologue* noted some 1.452 billion speakers of English worldwide in 2022,[3] with more than 1 billion speaking English as a second language.

Given the multiplicity of meanings and potential for confusion, educators working with international and immigrant families are recommended to take the following cautionary steps:

• Provide more context than you assume might be necessary. This could include explaining how tests are used in your mathematics class, the way in which you grade essay assignments, or why you find your approach helpful to the student's learning. The better foundations you are able to place, the better chance you have of narrowing the scope of language use.

• When conveying important information, explain your message twice, using different vocabulary each time. This will help second language speakers navigate any false friends and homonyms contained in your regular speech.

• Provide ample space for family members to discuss your message internally. With respect and empathy, ask them to explain their understanding of your message back to you as a means of checking comprehension. They may use a false friend or use a word that sounds accurate but may not accurately capture what you were trying to convey, so it's best to clarify parts that could be spots for confusion. For example, you may say that you wanted to focus on their child more. However, this could be interpreted as a promise to provide "special treatment," making it more essential to clarify what you mean, which could mean to work with the child more.

CULTURE

This section looks at research on the clusters of values in different geographic and cultural groupings. As we analyze the research, it is important to fight our natural tendency for stereotyping.

VALUES UNDERLYING OUR WORLDVIEW

Political scientists Ronald Inglehart and Christian Welzel are well known for their in-depth explorations of social and political change referenced as the "grand theory."[4] According to Inglehart and Welzel, one of the major fundamental changes occurring around the world is in the belief systems of people. The world is shaped by an interaction between the forces of socioeconomic development and persisting cultural traditions. Moreover, these changes influence mass values and produce growing pressures for establishing and strengthening democracy. The authors argue that socioeconomic modernization, rising liberty aspirations, and the quest for democratic institutions all reflect a common underlying human development process resulting in the broadening of human choice.

Their work is largely based on the annual World Values Survey, an international research program dedicated to scientifically examining social, political, economic, religious, and cultural values of people in the world. Conducted in waves every five years, this survey provides evidence of the persistence of distinctive cultural traditions within different geographic/ cultural groupings (see Figure 3.1).

The authors use this map to depict graphically their findings of two major dimensions of cross-cultural variation in the world.

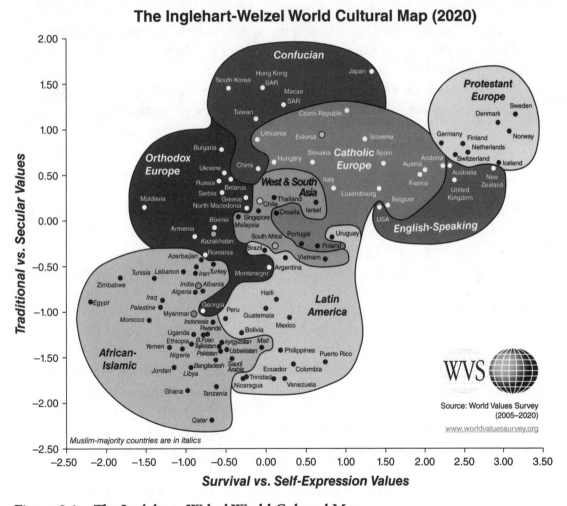

Figure 3.1   The Inglehart–Welzel World Cultural Map

Source: Inglehart–Welzel World Cultural Map—World Values Survey 7. http://www.worldvaluessurvey.org/.

1. Traditional values versus secular-rational values
2. Survival values versus self-expression values

   Traditional values emphasize the importance of religion, parent-child ties, deference to authority, and traditional family values. People who embrace these values also reject divorce, abortion, euthanasia, and suicide. These societies have high levels of national pride and a nationalistic outlook. Families coming from or identifying with these cultures may express initial suspicion of movements toward gender identity and social justice.

   Secular-rational values have the opposite preferences to the traditional values. These societies place less emphasis on religion, traditional family values, and authority. Divorce, abortion, euthanasia, and suicide are seen as relatively acceptable. (Suicide is not necessarily more common.)

   Survival values place emphasis on economic and physical security. It is linked with a relatively ethnocentric outlook and low levels of trust and tolerance.

   Self-expression values give high priority to environmental protection, growing tolerance of foreigners, gays and lesbians and gender equality, and rising demands for participation in decision-making in economic and political life.[5]

The map shows the scores of societies for these two dimensions. Going upward on this map demonstrates the shift from traditional values to secular-rational and going rightward shows the shift from survival values to self-expression values.

The researchers use groupings on the map to demonstrate how differences along these axes between societies follow a distinct clustering pattern of relation to cultural/geographic zones. East Asian societies with a historical basis for Confucian-oriented ways of being place a strong weight on secular-rational values, with some interesting variance on the axis of survival and self-expression. Islamic-African countries place by far the strongest emphasis on traditional values and survival values, while Northern Europe's Protestant societies demonstrate a high orientation toward secular-rational values and self-expression values.

This map further demonstrates the socioeconomic development of a country is linked with a broad syndrome of distinctive value orientations. We see that an increase in standards of living followed by post-industrial knowledge is correlated with higher societal orientation toward self-expression and secular-rational values. In further research, Inglehart argues the degree to which basic survival is secure dictates the values and behaviors of a society. In situations of extreme scarcity and competition for resources, distrust of outsiders and adherence to firm hierarchical rule is a valid strategy. Conversely, in societies that have achieved a level of material wealth to enable the majority of their population to feel economically secure, openness to ideas around alternative ways of life and social patterns becomes more possible.

An immediate and natural reaction to this research advises caution around making too much of these societal differences, as individual variance on values, which could be even greater, exists within societies. However, subsequent analysis by the World Values Survey researchers[6] found that the between-societal differences in values were 5 to 10 times as large a magnitude as those differences within societies.

This somewhat counterintuitive point can be illustrated through four fictional but archetypal individuals:

Thomas, a middle-aged American. Thomas grew up and was educated in New York City, and has spent the majority of his career working in the financial district. He considers himself something of a globalist, and has traveled widely.

Nirut, a Thai executive at an international financial company. Having grown up in Bangkok, he studied in the United States for both college and graduate school, and currently works in a global format, traveling frequently and interacting daily with people from around the world.

Nantawan, a Thai teacher who grew up in the northeast Isaan region of Thailand. Though she maintains a working knowledge of global affairs, Nantawan has little opportunities for interaction with foreigners, with her focus primarily on her students and immediate family.

Jeffrey, an older American farmer in Nebraska. Raised in the Midwest, Jeffrey has little interest in global affairs, though he maintains an active presence in his local community, serving several terms in the town government.

Despite the differences in personal living conditions, education, and other socioeconomic constructs, the research from the World Values Survey suggests that Nirut and Nantawan, and Thomas and Jeffrey are more likely to have similar values than would Thomas and Nirut.

Like most research, these findings can be taken with a grain of salt—however, educators should remain mindful of the lasting impact of initial conditions, and not assume an immigrant family has necessarily altered their values as a result of changing their country of residence.

MAINTAINING AWARENESS OF STEREOTYPES

Most educators are aware of the negative impact of stereotyping, and most schools actively seek to avoid practices that predetermine judgments or reactions based on assumptions about a particular individual, the individual's race, ethnicity, culture, etc.

That said, despite their bad reputation, the use of stereotypes has a demonstrable evolutionary advantage—being able to make rapid categorizations (even when faulty) allows people to move forward when faced with complexity or incomplete information.

Stereotyping is, in fact, an offshoot of the natural cognitive process known as social categorization, through which we automatically classify (and reclassify) individuals into social groups. This categorization can occur not only through racial, age, or gender characteristics, but also by profession, geography, or class. Social categorization occurs at such a deep level within our brains that it can take active and intentional thought to stop thinking about others in terms of their social groups.

It is vital to be aware of this innate tendency when engaging with students and others from international backgrounds and immigrants, and be cautious of the possibility that cultural stereotypes can hinder effective communication, teaching, and relationship building. Many researchers focus on cultural and linguistic stereotypes, primarily through the study of typical images and cultural clichés. These stereotypes highlight beliefs, attitudes, and prejudices of a particular community, region, and country. Each culture has special and unique characteristics, and thus their share of stereotypes—both positive and negative.

Some of the most common cultural stereotypes are:

- People from country A are better than people from country B.
- People from country A are all ignorant and rude.
- People from country A are less educated than people from country B or C.
- People from country A hate people from countries B and C.
- People from country A are violent and uncivilized.
- People from country A are musically inclined and great dancers.
- People from country A are lazy and disorderly.
- People from country A are well organized and on time.
- People from country A are the most efficient and innovative.
- People from country A are warm and welcoming.
- People from country A are all tall and gorgeous.
- People from country A are all smart and talented.

Educators who classify a student into one of these groups run the distinct risk of failing to provide proper individual support and scaffolding necessary for learning. For example, a teacher who subscribes to the Model Minority myth assumes that an Asian student "just has it" regarding geometry may fail to recognize a real struggle with understanding; or a coach who assumes a German student prioritizes timeliness may fail to help that student manage his executive functioning skills.

Being cognizant of our tendency to rely on cultural stereotypes is part of the skill set known as "intercultural competence." Educators who are able to mindfully and actively counter their "natural impulse" for social categorization will have more effective communications and collaborations with all students and families with whom they interact.

STEPS FORWARD

This section provides guidance for educators to move forward in light of the linguistic and cultural factors considered previously. This is, of course, not easy to do, and mistakes should be seen as opportunities for growth!

We begin with some general tips for structuring parent-teacher conferences, and then turn to fine-grained nuances of communications that can set the right tone for working together.

PARENT-TEACHER CONFERENCES

Parent-teacher conferences are the optimal setting for both parties to get to know each other and effectively assess the child's growth and development.

Ideally, a parent-teacher conference should include

- Sharing academic progress and growth based on classroom observations.
- Sharing and discussing testing data, assessments, portfolios, and assignments.
- Sharing and discussing the child's areas of strength and growth outside of academics.
- Learning more about the child from their parents or guardians.
- Discussing enrichment strategies to support students' learning and issues that may be interfering with their learning and growth.

General tips to keep in mind when conducting a parent-teacher conference with international or immigrant families are as follows:

Clarify role of teacher
Even before parent-teacher conferences, if your school works with many multicultural families, it's a good idea to have a warm letter of the teacher's role sent out in different

languages to better manage expectations. The role or expectations and perceptions of a teacher is often different in various cultures.

Prepare yourself

Make a list of items you want to raise with students' parents and write out what you know about the family background (and what assumptions you have).

Send an agenda

Write down a list of discussion topics to send to parents in advance, if possible in their own language. This is particularly useful for parents whose first language is not English, as it provides a framework for subsequent conversations.

Have a translator

If you have students and parents who have different language backgrounds, arrange a culturally fluent translator for better and more effective communication. Students and siblings are often asked to serve as translators, but this can result in inaccurate or misleading information being conveyed. It also keeps the burden on the students and forces them to be cultural brokers, which they may not be fully equipped or have time to do. As some parents may be illiterate, verbal conversation is the most effective.

Be welcoming

Welcome parents with a positive attitude and encourage them to ask questions. Be aware that your friendly attitude may not be reciprocated entirely, depending on the culture. The goal is for you to be conscious, empathic, and receptive toward others' cultural norms, not to subjugate your own. Some teachers set up a bowl of a popular sweet on their desk to show their attempts to be welcoming and providing a comfortable, familiar environment.

Listen actively

Pay close attention to what parents have to say about their child and incorporate this information into your teaching style accordingly. Ask questions and respectfully demonstrate curiosity about the home environment!

Allocate time *and* demonstrate flexibility

It is generally best to allot longer fixed time slots for parents who need translations during the course of the conference period. Make sure you provide alternatives for additional follow-ups and feedback about the child's progress. It can be valuable to open these channels as in-person, by phone, and over text formats, to provide space for parents' preferred communication methods.

(Gently) Give concrete examples of areas of growth and ask questions about misbehaviors

The term "disrespectful" can spark a lot of turmoil for families from East Asian and Middle Eastern backgrounds (and others). Instead of giving your interpretation of the student's intention, be as factual as possible, giving statements like "Luke is often quiet" or "he can go more than an hour without speaking in class."

From there, create the space to ask the family about where the behavior might be coming from. This is a wonderful opportunity to learn more about the student, the family dynamic, and even its history.

Parents will have a greater sense of trust and gratitude if they know you're helping their child with a weakness rather than just pointing it out. For parents who are not as familiar with the schools their children attend or not culturally or linguistically fluent in the main language used in the school, they may feel more lost on how to support the children. They may even subconsciously place a greater expectation on the role of the teacher.

For example, if your student is one who doesn't talk much in class, and it has been affecting the expectations you have for students, the following could be helpful.

Show the children a nonconfrontational/non-spotlight way to participate in class. You could start by having a game as an icebreaker where all need to participate.

For example, give students a multiple-choice question verbally, having students put their fingers up to show the response: One finger for the first response, two fingers for the second, and so on, and a fist if you don't know.

The first question should be a fun "gimme," such as: Is Ms. Brito 1) tall, 2) small, 3) a math teacher, 4) a young teacher? Continue with a few more, some of which can be related to course content or learning points you want to make.

In almost all situations, the students never fail to participate. After a few of these rounds, the shyest student may be the most active. Following up with direct questions about why the student chose the answer can continue the momentum for engagement.

A tangible example like this will reassure the parents you are being creative and helping their child have a voice in the class. You could also provide a way they can help keep up the momentum for the children at home.

Giving parents some of these reasons to help reassure them you are trying to understand (and therefore help solve) the challenges their children are having will often be greatly appreciated and respected.

To have truly culturally responsive conversations, the parents need to understand the situation at school and not just have teachers respond in a culturally respectful way. The parents then can at least understand the above reasons, for example, when they may never have thought of these reasons. You're equipping the parents, as well, with tools so they can have deeper conversations. You are also showing to them that you are working hard as a member of the "village" to raise the child, or in this case, teach the child.

As some parents do not speak English, using apps to help teachers and parents manage translations can be essential. Parent Square, ClassDojo, and TalkingPoints are three that some teachers say they find helpful.

This book recommends that educators advocate within their school for administrators to provide teachers with translators for both normal and difficult parent conversations. In some school districts, a simple click on a home page of the school brings teachers into direct connection with a real-time online translator. While resource constraints are certainly a reality, the importance of getting information across cannot be overstated.

CONFRONTING INITIAL ASSUMPTIONS

Teacher-parent communication can include many assumptions when dealing with domestic and international students. These assumptions vary based on the cultures of those involved the conversation. You can assume that both teachers and parents want to make the child successful, but there can be other subjective assumptions, too. A teacher expecting a student to vocalize their opinion to add their share of value is an example of an assumption. If a student is from a culture where this behavior isn't expected, this assumption can confuse them and make them feel directionless if they have not received the proper guidance. Additionally, if a student is from a different country and isn't White, some teachers have assumed the student and parents do not speak English. One teacher thought a parent who identified as West Indian didn't speak English. She spoke more slowly at first and offended the parent, as she was raised in a predominantly English environment in the island context.

One teacher with whom we worked found it valuable to write out his assumptions around the parent's knowledge of daily life in the school, time spent supporting the student at home, and knowledge of the subject matter sometime before parent-teacher meetings. He then became more aware of his own biases and was better able to frame his questions. He recognized the meeting required a level of delicacy in communications so as not to appear condescending or threatening.

When sitting with the parents, this teacher found it useful to say, "I know this is probably wrong, but since some parents found it difficult to . . . , I thought I'd check in with you. . . ."

Assumptions often come from a lack of understanding of the significance of different cultural events or celebrations. For example, a school in Massachusetts held its most significant state testing during Ramadan. After many petitions by the families, the school realized it needed to make accommodations. Administrators changed some of their policies to support them in the way they needed. In a related example, a teacher noticed that some of her students would not eat during lunch. She asked why and they said they were fasting during Ramadan. She asked if they wanted to sit in her classroom during lunch and they felt relieved. When she texted the parents through a translation app, the parents felt very grateful and started to have a good relationship with the teacher as well as a sense of community.

By actively and intentionally allowing assumptions to be checked amongst stakeholders, the space is created for a more authentic and respectful collaboration.

In the spirit of being co-problem-solvers with parents, setting a list of expectations and classroom behaviors but mentioning it as how you're creating a safe space show you're aware of their cultural gestures and its meaning and you'll support students to extend their culture and get to know another, which is vital in the success of their education. You could ask parents to let their children know that by engaging with eye contact in this classroom setting, they are showing curiosity, respect, and engagement. If you indicate you will also echo this, then you now have a team, which will amplify the message to the students.

PARENT-TEACHER NIGHTS

Some of the above solutions to parents can also be addressed in presentations to the families as a whole. During parent-teacher nights, if most of the parents speak another language and are not fluent in English, having a translator or a teacher who speaks that language conduct the presentation can be a powerful way to demonstrate respect and caring.

If there's a pattern of low parent turnout, try to find out through consistent but respectful inquiry for the reason. In one school, teachers found that parents were not attending due to the need to balance feeding their children and getting back to work at night. The school provided a small meal, which allowed parents to bring their children to the parent-teacher night, take care of dinner, and get back to their night shift all in one shot.

DEFINING SUCCESS

Success is a highly subjective term, and each individual student needs to learn and decide on the definition that resonates most with their personal and familial values. In the early stage of childhood development, the role of the teacher can be focused on helping students have a strong sense of self, empathy, social responsibility, and global citizenship.

Many cultures associate success with numbers. For example, a student's success is defined by their rank, GPA, and other scores. To extend this further, when teachers from different countries tell parents that their children are successful, they can mean very different things. One poignant example of this came early in our teaching career at an international school and discussing the relative difficulty of test items. The American teachers, by and large, considered passing marks to be over 80%, while a South African thought tests should be structured so the most capable students would achieve no higher than 50% at the most.

For educators helping international families to navigate the U.S. context, it can be critically important to impart the message that success at most American schools is not limited to academic performance and grades. Success can also mean how a child performs in extracurricular activities, including athletics and the arts, or their involvement in school government, or how they socialize with others.

Many people in various cultures, especially those who have attended more traditional school settings where extra and co-curriculars are not offered, could think of school as only a place to pursue academics. The soft skills learned from socializing with others may or may not resonate with the families but what's more is they may not even be aware the school offers such opportunities. For example, a Korean immigrant family asked why the teacher was advising their son to play sports and go to social functions, as this would take significant time away from what they perceived to be more important academic preparations. The family advised the son not to engage in such activities and that schoolwork was the most important.

This lack of exposure can also lead to pleasant surprises, of course. One Russian immigrant family came from a public school in Moscow. They were surprised to learn that embedded in the programs in the U.S. school were sports, arts, and clubs, and that some were even offered during the school day. They were excited to see that their children could have other ways to engage in the new school setting.

A recommended activity is to ask both parents and students to write out of their definitions of what would constitute a "successful academic year" and their reasons for why they believe this to be so. It may be helpful for the educator to do one as well. The educator can then facilitate a conversation around trade-offs and how different paths can lead to the achievement of the same goal, such as a focus on dramatic arts leading to a stronger college application.

Conversations around success can be sensitive among families, and educators should be ready to play the role of a facilitator and peacemaker.

CULTURAL PERSPECTIVE ON GIVING COMPLIMENTS

There is a general belief that if a person is feeling awkward, anxious, or denies a compliment, it is because they have low self-esteem or a negative self-image. However, when dealing with students from multiple cultures, teachers need to understand that praising an individual may not always have the desired effect.

Compliments, praise, and accolades have a large cultural and ideological component. For example, there are many cultures where it is common and acceptable to praise a child for their small achievements. However, other cultures have an implicitly understood ethos of crediting all achievements to a larger group, situations, or spiritual deity. Others may choose simply to avoid the conversation when somebody praises them.

Perhaps the best illustration of this came from our work with a Japanese family who moved to the United States when their children were in elementary school. A compliment from their child's art teacher expressed that Riyako was "a unique individual whose work clearly stands out from the rest of the students."

However, these parents had been inculcating their children with a strong value on humility and communal support, following the widely known Japanese proverb "the nail that stands up gets hammered down." The art teacher's compliment came across as a reason for shame, and they felt they needed to apologize to the teacher, which gave rise to a decidedly awkward conversation.

In another instance, a teacher praised her Indian student for the wonderful contributions he was making in the class. Immediately, the parent started to dispel and redirect the compliment by bringing up how others are doing the same or have other recognizable achievements. For example, the parent said, "Oh yes but I heard from my son that Michael is also doing just as great." Though this differs for individuals, if someone is receiving too many accolades, it can often be seen that the praise will actually "jinx" their success, especially because there is a belief that most people offering praise may not be 100% genuine.

For some students, being praised in class may make them feel uncomfortable because they don't want to show off or appear boastful, such as some Native Americans. When speaking with parents of some cultures, especially those that are more collectivistic, it's important to know that the parents may feel the same way when the teacher praises the student to them. When a parent dismisses the compliments, it's not because they are not happy about their child's performance but because it is culturally appropriate for them to do so.

In one instance, when Marina was translating for a Korean parent at one of the parent-teaching meetings, the teacher raved about the child, remarking on going beyond expectations: getting straight As, helpful in class, actively discussing with other students, what a great personality, etc. Marina could tell the mother beamed with pride and joy. She could not have been any happier. Marina then was tasked to translate the following:

"Oh really, well, (a sigh), it's because of you I'm sure that he's doing so well. Without you, there's no way he would be able to do well. It's all thanks to you. If it were up to him alone, he isn't a child who can do well. He's working hard because you've helped him find his motivation. It's all because of you."

Or in another meeting with a different Korean parent and in a different school, but similar genuine praise.

"Oh no, no you're wrong. He's not a who that does well. He needs to study harder."

There are countless cases like this. The parents deflect or deny the praise and the teachers get confused and at times concerned thinking the parents are putting too much pressure on the students. This assumption is also reinforced by the stereotype of Asian "tiger" parents. Marina explained to the parents what was actually going on, that the parents were truly beaming and would no doubt serve the child's most favorite dinner that night and speak with their husbands with joy filled in their hearts.

A BETTER USE OF *GOOD*

The word "good" is quite common in the educational world. It is highly associated with teachers praising students. However, the word "good" can have different meanings and associations in different cultures.

In cultures that have a more survivalist set of values, when a teacher says that a child is doing "well," an inadvertently offensive message can be conveyed that their child can't do any better.

We have seen countless conversations between parents from backgrounds highly attenuated to academic success (East Asian and Slavic, among others) and American educators follow these lines:

Teacher: Your child is doing well! I'm very pleased with her grades.
Parent: That's very good to hear. She works very hard.
Teacher: Yes, she does. You should be proud!

The teacher continues to praise the positive attributes of the child, but the parent later finds out that the student was getting a B. Thinking back to this conversation could be upsetting or disappointing for those parents whose linguistic mindset equates "doing well" or "good" to "getting the top grade." The teacher who provides this seemingly contradictory statement in the parent's mind could then be considered as lacking credibility and perhaps failing in efforts to support the student to perform at their true capacity. There is trust lost because the parent would have seen this time as a lost opportunity for the child to improve and learn more knowledge or skills.

Given this drive for continued improvement and success, we have seen conversations with Korean families that represented a true surprise for the educator:

Teacher: Your child is amazing! He's proactive in the class and often with correct answers. He is one of the most intelligent boys in the class.
Parent: Oh, he's not that great. He can study more and do a lot better.

In this case, a teacher may think that parents are being overly harsh with their son and become worried about the effect on the child's psyche. In the reality of the cultural construct of their own family, however, the Indian parents were extremely proud of their daughter, and simply felt it to be "good manners" to publicly decline compliments.

This wish to move beyond "good" is true of many families from Asian and Middle Eastern backgrounds, but can also emerge amongst many parents with similar educational values or who could behave similarly to any one of these scenarios.

One strategy we have seen be successful for educators who wish to engage with these families is to always be ready to lay out "improvement areas," regardless of the level of achievement. This focus on "what else needs to be done" provides the space to be taken seriously as an evaluator and supporter of talent and fulfills the expected role of a teacher.

THANK YOU

As mentioned earlier, there is a large cultural and ideological component to compliments. In many cultures, it's taught not to accept compliments even when they are genuine.

Korean culture, for example, is dominated by collectivism, meaning many Koreans tend to develop a strong in-group identity and view in-the-group as an extension of self. This tendency is well reflected in Confucianism, which highlights the importance of family, clear hierarchical relationships, and obedience to authority.

In Korean culture, as well as in other high-context or collectivist cultures, people deflect or deny the compliment to avoid appearing arrogant and to show modesty or humility, as the examples show. Many Koreans are more likely to give credit to the people who are in authority or express their achievement as collective efforts rather than as personal achievement.

One of this book's authors (Marina) remembers poignantly an array of guests praising her mother's cooking, only for her mother to provide a withering set of self-criticisms around the level of spice and crispness. Her mother adroitly turned each compliment into a self-deprecating issue, a graceful exercise perfectly in line with Korean values.

In Finnish culture, despite the value placed on self-expression, most parents never compliment their children because they think their child will become too proud, rude, and arrogant. Moreover, Finns generally don't smile without any reason, and if you smile at people without any reason, they may consider it weird. When you compliment, they are more likely to say things that sideline your compliment, but when they praise you, they mean it.[7] In Australia, meanwhile, when you compliment someone, they may feel like you are taunting them or do not mean what you are saying. They may also feel you are being sarcastic.[8] On the other hand, if you compliment someone in the United States, you are likely to expect to receive "thank you" as a response; if you don't receive this acceptance, it can feel like an insult to the person offering the compliment or a lack of confidence in yourself.

One key illustrative example of this came from Marina's middle school experience. Her White American teacher complimented her and said her hair looked particularly shiny and beautiful that day. Ture to her Korean roots, where compliments are humbly denied, Marina said, "Oh no, not at all. Not at all!"

The teacher responded, "Sweetie, if someone gives you a compliment, then you need to accept it gracefully by saying 'thank you.'"

Later that day, when at the dinner table, Marina's mother said, "Mina, you look particularly pretty today." Marina, remembering the lesson earlier, said, "Thank you" in Korean.

Her brothers cracked up laughing, jokingly saying, "Oh! So, you *do* think you are so pretty?" pointing out to her that she was so conceited. They continued saying, "You're not supposed to say that, silly. You're supposed to deny it. Don't you know anything?"

There are a few layers to this story.

First, the different cultural norms of how to receive compliments and to some extent whether compliments should be given in the first place as it may not be received as intended. There's a cross-cultural crossing of wires that happens.

The second, there's an implied cultural value—you're not supposed to think you possess positive attributes: beauty, intelligence, athleticism, kindness, etc. This is not about having confidence or not, although it can appear as if it does. Humility is what's encouraged.

Third, students who hear conflicting messages may be confused. Some students who hear one thing from parents and another from a teacher, two main sources of guidance, can be confused on what is proper behavior, not yet realizing there is not necessarily a right or wrong.

Seth vividly recalls an episode of this after leading a U.S. high school trip in Japan that involved an exchange between baseball teams. During a mixed scrimmage, the American coach told one of the Japanese players under his care that he was "throwing real heat." The player stared back blankly, gave a short nervous bow, and finally turned away. The coach was completely baffled, and this interaction sparked lengthy conversations between all educators at the end of the day. It became a great learning moment of differences in culture and values, or more accurately, perhaps, a difference in the manifestation of a value that we have categorized as a culture.

For educators in school settings, it can be helpful to be prepared to hear responses to compliments about their child from parents, "No, no, he's not doing that well. He could be doing better" or "It's all thanks to you" instead of accepting the compliment and saying thank you as mentioned earlier.

If the compliments are directed back to you, try to humbly mention that you are just doing your job, and thank them for giving you the pleasure to work with their student, while moving on to the next topic.

If the parent denies the complement, just thank them for giving you the pleasure to work with their child, and move on to the next topic.

This type of response can serve as a signal to educators that the parents place a high cultural value on humility, and thus help to steer the conversation toward areas of improvement.

SUMMARY

This chapter reviewed how differences in cultural cognitive framing can manifest in differences in language use. Therefore, understanding requires more than a "dictionary," but an understanding of the underlying value system. We looked at research from the World Values Survey, and then moved through a variety of practical tips and anecdotes for how to make stronger relationships with parents and impart information clearly. For translation tools and apps, Parent Square, ClassDojo, and TalkingPoints have been helpful for many teachers.

SELF-REFLECTIVE EXERCISES FOR EDUCATORS

- Watch a movie that focuses on a school environment in a culture different from your own. Take notes on the behaviors of students, teachers, and parents. Even if the plots and situations are exaggerated, you would still be able to get past that and assess the value.

- Write out the agenda for your most successful parent-teacher conference. What alterations would you make if the parents were from a society with high survivalist values? With high self-expression values?

- Write out a way in which you commonly provide praise to a student's parents. Try to come up with alternative phrases that convey the intended meaning in different cultural responses.

- Consider your own personal levels of comfort around praise and compliments (both giving and receiving). Where did your sense of what is "right" come from?

NOTES

1. Boas, F. (1911). Handbook of American Indian Languages. Bureau of American Ethnology, Bulletin 40. Washington DC: Government Print Office. Smithsonian Institution, Bureau of American Ethnology 1: pp. 1–83.
2. Lucy, J.A. (2001). Sapir-Whorf hypothesis. International Encyclopedia of the Social & Behavioral Sciences, pp. 903–906.
3. Ethnologue. (2022). What are the top 200 most spoken languages? https://www.ethnologue.com/guides/ethnologue200 (accessed 22 September 2022).
4. Inglehart, R. and Welzel, C. (2005). *Modernization, Cultural Change, and Democracy: The Human Development Sequence*. New York: Cambridge University Press.
5. World Values Survey. (2022). Overview. https://www.worldvaluessurvey.org/wvs.jsp (accessed 22 September 2022).
6. World Values Survey. (2022). Catalogue of Findings. https://www.worldvaluessurvey.org/wvs.jsp (accessed 22 September 2022).
7. Holmes, J. and Brown, D. (1987). Teachers and students learning about compliments. *TESOL Quarterly* 21 (3): pp. 523–546.
8. Winch, G. (2013). Why some people hate receiving compliments: how self-esteem influences our capacity to receive praise. *Psychology Today* (27 August).

4

STAYING MINDFUL
OF NUANCES

Decades of research show that parental involvement in their child's education is a vital component for their academic success. For this reason, the U.S. federal government has enacted two critical policies in this regard. The No Child Left Behind Act, established in 2001, specifies that meaningful communication between parents and teachers is an important aspect of a student's achievement. Then, in 2015, the Every Student Succeeds Act called for the use of federal funds to promote parental engagement with their child's school.

However, not all communication is good communication. When teachers talk with parents, the words they use matter, as discussed in previous chapters. This is especially true when communicating with families of different ethnic, cultural, national, and geographic backgrounds. Word choice often causes unintended consequences. As previously noted in Chapter 3, with compliments and assessment of ability, the underlying connotations of words can create a rift during exchanges between parents and educators.

Unfortunately, specific training in parent-teacher communication and all of its nuances is uncommon. The task then falls on the teacher to bridge this gap. Teachers must proactively strive to communicate with parents of varying multicultural backgrounds effectively. This can have a positive impact on academic achievement; a 2009 in-depth analysis on public schools in Michigan[1] demonstrated that greater trust within a school community is associated with increased school achievement on assessments for mathematics and reading.

Becoming more conscious of the ways different word choices impact parent-teacher relationships can help build trust, which often translates to raising a student's academic achievement.

One goal throughout the book is to help teachers better understand how the words they use can impact their relationships with parents. The chapter will provide background information about word choice concerning specific ethnic and cultural groups and targeted strategies to forge stronger partnerships between teachers and parents.

MANAGING CONVERSATIONS WITH DIFFERENT ETHNIC, CULTURAL, AND GEOGRAPHIC GROUPS

The meaning of a word can easily change depending on with whom you are talking. The way a person interprets a word is often influenced by their particular cultural lens. As noted in Chapter 3, using what might seem like a normal word like "thanks" can create a barrier or raise tensions between a parent and a teacher. Addressing these barriers is a cornerstone to building stronger partnerships between teachers and parents, which will, in effect, have a positive impact on the students.

Teachers desire to make their interactions with parents as productive as possible but the parents may not always perceive it to be so. When a teacher uses a certain word in conversations with parents of different ethnic groups, it can create tension without the teacher realizing it. For example, on a student evaluation following a travel program, school staff noted that a Turkish student "could have demonstrated more respect to the tour guides," intending to give a gentle nudge to improve the student's behavior. However, given the high importance placed on demonstrating veneration in traditional Turkish culture, the use of "respect" resulted in a significant escalation, fracturing the relationship between student, educator, and parents. These misunderstandings are often unforeseen educational pitfalls that can be easily overlooked.

Productive conversations between teachers and parents can make a world of difference when managing student successes and instances of concern. If a parent misinterprets a teacher's comments because of a discrepancy in a word's meaning, the way they deal with their child can drastically change. Furthermore, it can also create mistrust between the parent and the teacher and/or between the teacher/parent and the student. In turn, this can impact student success.

In one instance, a ninth-grade female student from Shanghai was sitting with her mother in a parent-teacher conference. The student was close to her Spanish teacher, and she confided in the teacher about a lot of things going on in her life, including a crush she had on a boy sitting next to her in class. During the parent-teacher conference, the teacher jokingly said the student had a crush and maybe that's why she's so good in the class. To the teacher, her cultural norm was teens who date. However, her mother, who was used to and valued a different cultural norm, thought the teacher was implying that her daughter wasn't paying enough attention, and scolded her, making a connection to the Chinese expression *zǎo liàn*. This means "early love," and implies that youth should not be dating as they are not ready. The mother placed a closer eye on the girl's social life, restricting much of her freedom, and further emphasized her studying.

The student was angry at her teacher for telling her mother and putting her in a vulnerable situation she was not ready to tackle. In her view, the student had shown her American identity to the teacher but felt betrayed and became distrustful of the teacher. This incident hurt her relationship with the teacher for some time. The teacher did not learn about this mistake until a few months later and was devasted to learn about the issues she had caused.

In another instance, a Russian international student was surprised to hear the teacher would mention personal traits, like how funny the student was, to her parents. Both she and her parents were surprised. Parent-teacher meetings in Russia were never that personal. To this particular family, having come from what felt like an oppressive educational environment to them, such observations were refreshing. To others, however, it felt like a waste of time, and resulted in confusion at why the teachers would feel the need to comment on a student's personality. They wanted to know their child's performance and ways to improve if needed. Additionally, they felt they had less time with the teacher as other English-speaking families because of the time it took to interpret. There was a feeling the teacher was not efficient and a sense that the teacher was a bit flighty, and distrust started to form.

At times, some teachers prefer to have the student in the same room with the parent during a parent-teacher meeting. which can be a surprise for some families at first because of its democratic structure. Many of these students appreciate it if the teacher could first speak with the student on the topics to discuss, especially on an academic or behavioral matter, so they can help frame the content properly to the parent. As some students do have different identities in school and with their family, as in the case above, students can be prepared to respond to uncomfortable content.

For example, one teacher mentioned to the parent about how the student didn't speak much in class and thus grades were hurting. This school did not share extensive comments on student performance in reports. The student felt he was caught off guard, especially by the critical tone of the teacher. Instead of offering criticism, which can ignite an argument for the family, have an open conversation with the student. Otherwise, the perceived criticism could cause a meltdown that may have been prevented. Anxiety may run high regarding education in some cultures more than others, so being aware of this is important.

One way the teacher could have shaped the conversation was with a caring tone and words like, to the parent, "I love the content of his contributions in class." To the student, the teacher could say, "David, what do you think you can do to increase your contributions even more? Doing so in the way we've been discussing could get you an entire letter grade jump, although, of course, the most important thing is that we get to hear you and you get to listen to others share their thoughts."

Overcoming cross-cultural language barriers is particularly important when facing concerns about students' academic progress or behavior. Understanding how a parent's cultural value system could impact the way they interpret communications is, therefore, essential. Known as "social perspective taking" by psychologists, the intentional process of attempting to figure out what others are thinking and feeling and their perception about situations has had demonstrable positive impacts in many domains.

A notable study in this regard took place in 2009,[2] as the U.S. Army conducted research on training soldiers for social perspective taking in cross-cultural communications, as a reaction to ongoing challenges in Iraq and Afghanistan. The study's curriculum included supporting soldiers to be conscious of their propensity for perceptual biases, developing the habit of creating multiple hypotheses about other's perspectives, and checking in as much as possible on the validity of these hypotheses. With sufficient practice, the researchers found that soldiers could achieve automaticity in social perspective taking. They demonstrated that, even in situations where a common language was lacking, soldiers who utilized this process were able to effectively understand host-national goals while accomplishing U.S. missions and objectives.

A parent-teacher conference is certainly a different context, but the lessons of this study still apply. Teachers who make the effort and take a parent's perspective into consideration will have a better chance of communicating with them effectively.

One teacher interviewed for this book learned this the hard way, while working at a public school in Philadelphia. Her population of families were diverse, with a plurality of Black Americans, as well as first-generation immigrants from Uzbekistan, Bulgaria, China, Mexico, and the Dominican Republic. She was shocked when, during parent conferences with a family from the Dominican Republic, the mother told her that her daughter felt the teacher was racist. As she moved beyond the initial shock, the teacher probed into this perception, asking the parents to explain what the student had told them.

She found that an early event had had a large effect. During initial class icebreakers, the teacher had asked students to share a cultural tradition. When no one volunteered, she called first on a Bulgarian boy, and then a Uzbekistani girl to share. Both students provided great examples of their family holidays, and the teacher continued with her lessons, thinking she had done a good job of setting an inclusive atmosphere for her class.

For the Dominican student, however, the teacher had only tried to "include" students who looked "White," ignoring others in the class. During the parent conference, the teacher moved through the difficult conversation, explaining her intentions and apologizing for how her actions impacted the class dynamics.

After the parents agreed to speak with their daughter about this misunderstanding, the teacher replayed the icebreaker in her head, thinking about what she might have done differently. She realized that one root cause was failing to engage the majority of students in finding out about their peers. She came back to the exercise in the next class, asking students to engage in a "pair-and-share" exercise so that all backgrounds could be heard.

The bottom line is that teachers should be mindful of the words they use, the content and context, and the ways they communicate with parents and students with different ethnic, cultural, or national backgrounds. A Chinese parent might interpret a word differently than a Korean parent. A Mexican parent might take offense to a word that a Middle Eastern parent takes no note of. A chance remark like "your child occasionally gets distracted" may seem insignificant to the teacher, but could result in untold repercussions for the student.

With some students, school is a place they feel they can be their "American" self or at least to show a different identity than they have at home. When that gets shattered, students may no longer feel there is a place for them to express this side of them. Being mindful of words that might seem negligible, and instead shaping your choice of words use based on the background of families, matters.

As challenging as it is to be aware of various cultures and expectations, thoughtfully engaging in these processes improves; as one teacher put it, I want to be a better teacher, and I will get better and better with each interaction.

CULTURAL BACKGROUNDS

The background in which people are raised can play a significant role in how they interpret different words. Even the most minuscule shift from a teacher's use of one word to another can contribute to variations in interpretation on the part of the parent. The cultural background of a parent often influences their perception of words and what they mean in the context of their child's education.

It is well beyond the scope of this book to attempt to fully delineate the factors that differentiate cultural backgrounds that make up the modern United States, especially considering that even within a culture, there are variations dependent on regions and local history, to say the least. Also, within the variations, individuals' mindsets can shape the way they process information. Indeed, in terms of sheer numbers, the United States has far more immigrants than any other nation in the world, with well over 40 million people living in the United States who were born in another country. Based on 2015 estimates by the United Nations, nearly one in five of all international migrants live in the United States.[3]

As shown in Figure 4.1, Mexicans constitute the largest group of immigrants to the United States, nearing 25% of the overall foreign-born population in 2016, The next two immigrant groups were China and India, each at 6%. Other top nations of origin include the Philippines (5%); El Salvador, Vietnam, Cuba, and the Dominican Republic (3% each); and Guatemala and Korea (each 2%).

The following sections briefly describe those cultural backgrounds that constitute the highest populations in the United States, along with others that hold unique qualities that may cause them to interpret words in ways many teachers might not expect. It is fundamental to point out the diversity of cultures comprised in each of these groupings, as there are no singular set of ideas and values simply because nations may fall within similar geographic

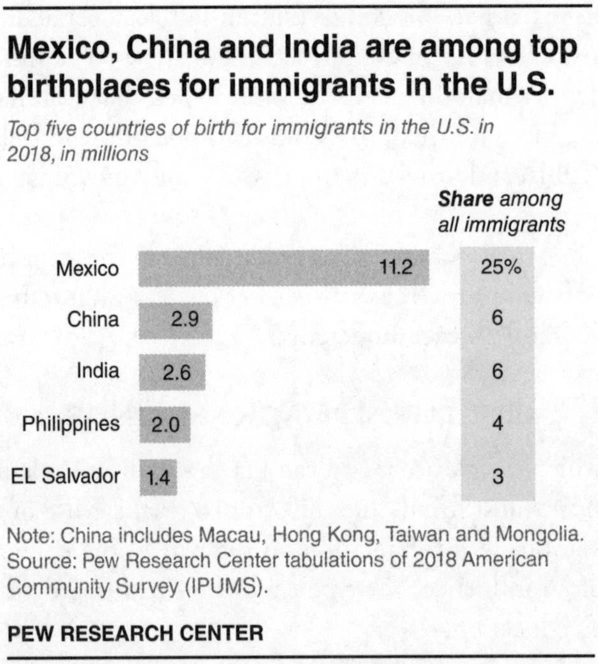

Mexico, China and India are among top birthplaces for immigrants in the U.S.

Top five countries of birth for immigrants in the U.S. in 2018, in millions

		Share among all immigrants
Mexico	11.2	25%
China	2.9	6
India	2.6	6
Philippines	2.0	4
EL Salvador	1.4	3

Note: China includes Macau, Hong Kong, Taiwan and Mongolia.
Source: Pew Research Center tabulations of 2018 American Community Survey (IPUMS).

PEW RESEARCH CENTER

Figure 4.1   Top birthplaces for immigrants in the United States.
Source: Pew Research Center. Key Facts about U.S. Immigration.

domains. Classifying one ethnicity or culture for another can negatively impact a parent's confidence and trust in a teacher.

These notes are intentionally succinct, and, therefore, written at a level of generalization that glosses over the nuances that make up the beauty of each culture. The authors acknowledge this inherent shortcoming of this work.

LATIN AMERICAN COUNTRIES

Latin America is commonly defined as all those parts of North, Central, and South America that were part of the Spanish, Portuguese, or French colonial empires. This includes Mexico in North America; Guatemala, Honduras, El Salvador, Nicaragua, Costa Rica, and Panama in Central America; Colombia, Venezuela, Ecuador, Peru, Bolivia, Brazil, Paraguay, Chile, Argentina, and Uruguay in South America; and Cuba, Haiti, the Dominican Republic, and Puerto Rico in the Caribbean. The variety of histories, ethnic groups, and races makes Latin America one of the most diverse in the world; this diversity should be seen as a driving reason for educators to make direct inquiries about the individual family's unique background.

Strong familial ties are often a predominant cultural trait in the entire region of Latin America. This is in part because of the collectivist societies of the region and also due to the dominance of Catholicism across the region. In many Latina/o homes, there is often a belief that if bad things happen, it was God's will. Family members tend to be conscious of their responsibilities to one another, and place a high priority on "showing up" for events like graduations, weddings, holidays, and reunions. In addition, many Latino parents tend to value obedience over independence in their children, as they come from a culture where respect for elders is paramount. There are often gender expectations for females to cook and clean and even work in high school. In some families, it wasn't uncommon to hear the parents saying to their child at the age of 15, "You are going to get a job." The same expectation of cooking and cleaning often doesn't exist for males, yet, in some Latino/a cultures, the pressure to be "machismo" is real.

There is often significant respect, like in many cultures, given to anyone in a titled position, such as therapists, counselors, or teachers.

Latinos/as across the board also tend to place great value on personal relations, meaning that approaching each other with warmth and enthusiasm is customary. Friends and family often greet each other with a kiss on the check. Vibrant conversations and lively debates are the norm. Having significant loyalty to each other, it's not uncommon to think of extended families as a close sibling or another parental figure.

Many Latin Americans consider themselves to be "proud people." On a macro level, this pride tends to focus on aspects of their home nation's culture, history, and geographic beauty, as opposed to political leadership and societal development. On the level of the individual family, Latin American pride can show up in intense celebrations of personal achievements and an ease with showing off one's wealth and health. It could also show in a parent refusing to have an interpreter for a parent-teacher meeting. Overprotectiveness of children can be a very common trait in many Latin American families, on occasion resulting in virulent debate at perceived slights from well-intentioned educators.

SLAVIC COUNTRIES

Slavic countries include Russia, the Czech Republic, Slovakia, Poland, Belarus, Ukraine, Bulgaria, Slovenia, Croatia, Serbia, Bosnia and Herzegovina, North Macedonia, and Montenegro. However, several other Eastern European countries, such as Romania and Armenia, have been highly influenced by Slavic culture because of former Soviet occupation and proximity.

In traditional Slavic culture, privacy is often highly valued, and people tend to be reserved and formal. The unyielding climate and history of oppressive regimes can lead many people of Slavic origins to have a skeptical and cynical outlook. In line with a preference for more survival values, many lean toward stable and predictable environments, with avoidance of new "innovations."

In many cases, a high value is placed on personal relationships and trust, with large degrees of suspicion toward anyone who is not well known. Blunt honesty is seen as an important character trait, leading to a general sense of "telling it like it is" and distrust of overly nuanced explanations. Familial relationships are highly important and many Slavic families are involved with each other's lives. Though generally aligned toward gender equality, in many Slavic households men are considered to be the main workers and providers, while women have primary responsibility for the home and children.

MIDDLE EASTERN COUNTRIES

Lacking a definitive geographic or political definition, the Middle East came into usage in the early 1900s in counterpoint to the "Far East" of Asia. A narrow conception of the Middle East comprises Bahrain, Cyprus, Egypt, Iran, Iraq, Israel, Jordan, Kuwait, Lebanon, Oman, Palestine, Qatar, Saudi Arabia, the Syrian Arab Republic, Turkey, the United Arab Emirates, and Yemen. The "Greater Middle East" has been used to include Afghanistan (though often categorized as a part of Asia), the Comoros, Djibouti, Maghreb, Pakistan, Sudan, and Somalia.

The Middle East stands as the birthplace of three of the world's major religious traditions: Judaism, Christianity, and Islam. As each of these religions drew on the same early texts, they share several rules and beliefs, including respect for civil law and a tradition of prophets.

Islamic traditions are commonly associated with the modern Middle East, and for many families of Middle Eastern background, Islamic rules governing conduct play a dominant role in daily life.

Privacy is highly valued, and many families will not discuss internal matters with outsiders. While customs differ and may be loosened among immigrant families, many women choose to wear hijab or a veil, or a burqa, which are robes that hide the outline of their bodies. The shoulders and arms are considered to be the most important areas to cover, and doing so can be a sign for educators that their religious beliefs and culture should be taken seriously.

Family is an integral aspect of Middle Eastern culture, with strong connections maintained between tribes and clans over time. Arabic honorific names can be used in preference to given names, as a man may be called Ibn ("son of") followed by his father's name or Abu ("father of") followed by his child's name. Strong family ties are a source of cultural pride, with an ages-old Arab adage expression being "I and my brothers against my cousins; I and my cousins against the stranger."[4] Values of respect, honor, and loyalty derive from these strongly connected extended families.

Gender roles in many Middle Eastern families can be highly stratified, with traditional home construction creating separate spaces for entertaining male and female guests. Many men are expected to play a patriarchal role, taking care of the family financially and feeling shame if incapable of doing so. Many women choose to maintain a traditional role, raising children and managing home affairs. While Western perceptions of the culture tend to stress the historical gender inequalities, traditions are changing. However, many families may be discreet about these changes, and still defer to the father for final say in decisions.

Education is highly valued, and many Middle Eastern parents, like in other cultures, are very proud of their children's academic accomplishments. Educators may be expected to demonstrate their own level of impression for the student's achievements, and (perhaps) help parents to celebrate.

East Asian Countries

The cultural sphere of East Asia actually contains several nations in both the geographic East and Southeast Asia that have a strong historical influence from Imperial China. These include modern-day China, Taiwan, Japan, Korea, and Vietnam; some scholars also include Thailand, Myanmar, Cambodia, Mongolia, and Singapore in this sphere of influence. As a dominant regional power, Imperial China exerted influence on its neighboring states, the interactions of which led to the flow of Confucianism, Buddhism, and Taoism across the region.

The continued influence of Confucianism may be the most notable element continuing to unite the cultures of these distinct nations. The civil examination model was a crucial vehicle of social mobility in Imperial China. It presented equal opportunities for all; even a young person from a poor family could join the ranks of the most educated elites by succeeding in the civil examination system. However, the assurance of success in this examination system depended on one's ability instead of social position. This approach helped circulate the core ideas of Confucianism—concerning proper relationships, behavior, rituals, and more.

The hope of social mobility through a successful Confucianism was the greatest motivation for going to school, whether the learner was the son of a farmer or a reputable scholar. Even for the farmer's child who didn't perform well enough to take the civil service examinations at the lowest level, going to school had a significant payoff of working literacy. This literacy was acquired through careful mastery of the basic texts that other learners who passed the exams at the highest level studied.

This level of curricular uniformity had a powerful influence on both Imperial Chinese society and its offshoots throughout East Asia. The significant impetus for this uniformity was an important meritocracy promoted by the civil service exam system. In its idealized state, this system recruited civil officials based on true merit instead of political or family connections. In reality, the system largely became a tool of the elite, with the benefits mostly conferred to the rich and powerful (and male) classes.

Despite these inherent inequities, the Confucian system provided a set of strict advisements and rules for maintenance of harmony in all aspects of a society, with great importance given to the perpetuation of hierarchical roles, a focus on group cohesion, and continued respect for elders. In traditional Confucianism, behaving according to your particular role is considered essential for keeping society harmonious. The individualism and personal preferences so highly prioritized by the West are deprioritized in the East, as the good of the group is seen as more important than the individual.

Following this preservation of harmony is an important concept known as "saving face." In this viewpoint, a well-mannered individual will go to great lengths to avoid embarrassing others. For educators unfamiliar with interactions with East Asian families, it may feel like the family is going to great lengths to avoid saying "no" directly. This can be due to an implicit expectation for the educator to pick up on unspoken cues and stop pushing, thereby saving the family from the embarrassment of saying no.

Research by cognitive scientists Richard Nesbitt and Takahiko Masuda[5] has shown that East Asians and Westerners effectively perceive very different worlds. In one experiment, East Asian and American graduate students were tasked with noting their observations of a virtual aquarium on a computer screen. The East Asian students primarily described the overall environment, including the color of the water, the rocks and shells used for decoration, and the relationship of all fish in the tank. The American students, meanwhile, noted the largest and most prominent fish first, describing them in great detail. The background context was not seen as nearly as important.

The researchers' main takeaways from this study were that East Asians live in a world where prescribed roles dictate how they navigate complex social networks, making attention to context paramount to success.

The national cultures of these East Asian nations, of course, have much variance, and delving deeply into the facets is beyond the scope of this work. We instead make some brief observations of China and South Korea, as the two East Asian nations with the highest percentage of foreign-born immigrants to the United States. Twentieth-century events in both countries have altered the structure of their government and society, and thus had an impact on the national cultures of each nation.

The influence of communism on Chinese values and behaviors should not be dismissed, as the stability of the governing party has provided the Chinese Communist Party with the ability to adopt a mindset for, arguably, planning that is far more than what Americans usually view as long term. This "long-view" perspective can show up in the behaviors and viewpoints of everyday Chinese. Similarly, the modern Chinese communist state has pushed forward a value of efficiency and practicality as cultural values, which can often show up as primary justification for decisions.

For modern South Korea, meanwhile, the aftereffects of the Korean War in the 1950s have had a lasting impact. The war left South Korea as a highly impoverished nation under constant threat of invasion from its neighbor to the north. From the 1960s to the 1980s, the country went through a period of rapid economic development, accompanied by pressures for financial success as important for societal progress. This ethos of "constant threat" and the need for self-sacrifice for one's family and nation have placed a value on hard work in modern Korean culture that could be unsurpassed in the world. Indeed, in 2019, Koreans worked 1,967 hours a year per employee, 241 hours more than the OECD average of 1,726 hours and 323 hours longer than their counterparts in Japan, which tallied 1,644 hours on average.

SOUTH ASIA (INDIA)

Tracing back over four millennia, the civilization developed on the subcontinent known as India is among the world's oldest and richest. A common refrain amongst Indians is to declare Indian culture to be *sa prathama sanskrati vishvavara,* the first and the supreme culture in all the world. Modern India is characterized by massive diversity, with its more than 1.3 billion people speaking 23 officially recognized languages. India is considered to be the birthplace of Hinduism and Buddhism, the third and fourth most widely followed religions in the world.

India has a long history of social stratification, often referred to as the "caste" system. Unique to the Indian subcontinent, there are two overlapping systems of castes. Under the larger varna system, society is classified into five broad categories: *brahmin* (priests), *kshatriya* (nobility), *vaishya* (merchants), *shudra* (laborers), and *dalits* (untouchables). On a more micro level, the *jati* is comprised of over 2,000 categories based on the family of birth that rank occupations and vocations.

While caste-based discrimination has been declared illegal in modern India, the social and cultural reverberations continue to influence aspects of daily life. Open prejudice may be generally frowned upon, but a subtle determination of the social position of oneself in relation to others is often present in many interactions. This commonly shows up in questions around professions and family history.

Many Indians generally maintain a strong relationship with their family, relatives, and members of their community. Many Indian Americans tend to socialize primarily with other Indian Americans, with over 80% of U.S.-born Indian Americans reporting a spouse or partner of Indian origin.[6] Many Indians tend to be quite conservative in their behavior and dress, and very few people wear revealing clothing. It is somewhat common for those of opposite genders to avoid physical contact.

It is difficult to overstate the enormous value placed on education within the Indian American community. From U.S. Census data, Indian Americans have substantially greater educational attainment than the mean U.S. household, as the share of Indian Americans completing college was roughly double the national average in 2020, leading to a similar advantage in standards of living. Many parents from Indian backgrounds can be extremely directive toward their children's academic and extracurricular pursuits. The cliché of Indian mothers choosing their children's college majors has some basis in reality, with a strong preference for STEM-based careers, followed by business and legal professions,[7] They set the bar extremely high for their children and tend to be strict, stemming from the home context of high population competing for scant resources.

THE PHILIPPINES

After the Philippines became a territory of the United States following the Spanish-American War in 1898, Filipinos began to immigrate in progressively larger numbers, with over 1% of the national population having some Filipino heritage by the 1970s.[8] Unlike many other countries in Asia, the Filipino culture demonstrates a strong influence from other nations, due to Spanish and American colonization, Japanese occupation, and ongoing trade with China, the Pacific Islands, Portugal, and Australia. The impact of colonialization in particular was severe in the Philippines, as changes in language and religion were enforced first by Spain and later by the United States. For many Filipinos, the colonial mentality resulted in a form of internalized oppression that results in a rejection of traditional practices in favor of a preference for anything "different." Given this history and blend of cultural influences, some historical researchers[9] posit that Filipino Americans are in fact bicultural, with the capacity to maintain beliefs, values, and behaviors of both their home and host country simultaneously.

That said, several cultural traits from the Philippines continue to influence the values of Filipino Americans. Most importantly are *utang na loob* (expression of gratitude), *pakikisama* (harmony), and *tsismis* (gossip). *Utang na loob* often is seen in the form of acts of kindness to other parties and is considered a reciprocal obligation where one act of benevolence creates a feeling of indebtedness on the other party. *Pakikisama* revolves around a spirit of respect toward members of one's family, particularly elders. In general, "elder" applies to all family members who are older, as they are considered to have enough wisdom and experience to provide astute advice. *Tsismis* is a friendly form of gossip that encourages the free flow of information within a family unit.[10]

For many modern Filipino Americans, religion is a dominant cohesive force, with the vast majority following the Catholic faith. This bonding force provides one hypothesis for research findings[11] showing that Filipino Americans identified more with Latino ethnic groups than Asian Americans. This may be because ideals of familial pride and love stemming from Spanish colonization influenced many Filipino individuals to develop similar values on warm interpersonal relationships.

NATIVE AMERICANS

Although in today's U.S. population, they are not a large minority group, it seemed remiss not to include them. Each Native American tribe has its own manifestations of values, including a strong respect for teachers. Most Native American tribes do not make eye contact with teachers and take it as a personal offense if a teacher or anyone else pats them on their heads or rubs the top of the heads. Within the Picayune Rancheria and other tribes, the students may stare at the left shoulder of the teacher instead. Additionally, when there's a reference to Native Americans, the first reference that one makes is to the tribe, then to Native American for many. For example, an Apache may state which Apache they are first, then note that they are Native American. Almost all tribes believe they were the first of the tribes to be on the planet, and perhaps reflecting this, respective tribes call themselves, translated, the People (Navajo, Yokuts, etc.). Teachers may work with families in one of the following types of schools: mission (run by local religion), tribal, a school a part of the Bureau of Indian Reservation Schools, and the local charter/public schools.

When working with a Native American family, it is ideal to find someone with whom you feel comfortable talking about the tribes. They can help you understand why children may miss school (e.g., rotations to live with grandparents/other relatives) or the tradition of Easter for some tribes, where the holiday is observed and celebrated for five to seven days 24 hours a day. Some tribes suffered tremendously over the centuries and part of the way they observe Easter is to sing. It's also important to understand the status of the child. For example, in some tribes, certain girls are vetted and selected for important ceremonials and have a bodyguard 24/7, 365 days a year. The girls, whose families are often highly reputable, have a very high status and importance to the tribe. In another example, a teacher had a young girl whose father was the Vice Chair of the Tribal Council, a very high position. The teacher was told not to joke around with her in the same way she would with the other students. Her classmates understood and showed similar respect, as well.

When talking with Native American parents, it's important to understand the status of the family and child as well as its ceremonial holidays. One teacher didn't realize the student would be missing a few weeks of school throughout the year. If she had known this, she would have worked with the parents to make sure the student could catch up in his work each time he came back.

It is important to keep in mind that each culture has different ways to show cultural traits like "strong familial ties," "respect for elders," or "an enormous value placed on education." Americans, as do many other peoples in the world, argue that their culture puts importance in all these values and such concepts are not isolated to one cultural group or another. However, it can seem as if there are not shared values. For example, when indicating that Asians show respect to their parents or elders, it does not mean that Americans do not. Respect to elders in a typical American family dinner conversation may consist of a debate. It could show to the elders that the children are thoroughly trying to understand the depth of the topic. For Koreans, respect may mean obedience and the expected response would be nods and an affirmative *neh*, which means "yes." It's not so much that the other cultures do not have similar values, such as respect or familial ties, but rather the manifestations of them and the contexts in which they are shown are nuanced.

During meetings with parents or when parents are visiting the school, it is essential to keep this complexity in mind when listening or responding to the words parents or interpreters use. A parent who says, "I think my child needs to be more respectful to you," may mean that the student should not make eye contact, which would be different than the teachers' expectations for the student. Asking follow-up questions on how they define respect would help clarify the expectations, keep messages to the student coming from both family and school consistent, and, therefore, better support the success of the student.

Today, many classrooms have wonderful celebrations of a culture in a classroom through flags, pictures of food, maps, and other tangible representations. Although it can be very important to show that the student's culture is represented in the classroom, it's also important to reflect the multicultural perspectives, or at least show the appreciation or complexity of them through conversations, which are already few and far between with some families and in some school systems.

LOW-CONTEXT AND HIGH-CONTEXT CULTURES

Cultures have also been categorized as having high-context or low-context (see Figure 4.2).

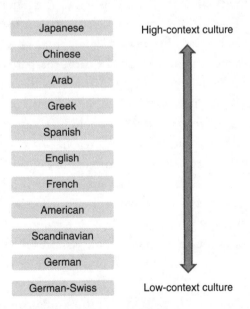

Figure 4.2   High-context and low-context cultures.
Source: Samovar and Porter, 1997, p. 24; Seuda and Fukuda, 2011, p.132.

Generally, high-context cultures (China, Korea, Saudi Arabia) are often collectivistic, where they place more value of an entire group than an individual, and have nonverbal cues, therefore having implicit communication, an example of which is the incidence where the mother asked Marina to teach her child about the birds and the bees. A low-context culture tends to be individualistic, rely on verbal cues, and explicitly communicate. Thus, how one communicates to the other, both verbal and nonverbal, can lead to successful or disastrous outcomes.

MAKING PROGRESS: CHOOSING WORDS CAREFULLY

Choosing the right words to use in conversations with people of different ethnic, cultural, or national backgrounds will depend on where they are from. With just a little bit of understanding about their culture, you can select words that will be effective for communication in each case. Even if you are talking to different parents about the same work or project, the specific words you use and the way you frame the conversation can either build or undermine trust.

As mentioned previously, a parent's cultural background may cause them to define words differently than you do. For example, as discussed in Chapter 3, using the word "good" in reference to a student earning a B might not be taken well by an Indian parent who values academic excellence. If the teacher thinks a B is good, the parent may start to doubt the teacher's credibility if the parent finds anything less than an A to be worthy of praise.

In this instance, the teacher's use of the word "good" may also indicate to the parent that they think this is the best the student can do. In turn, the parents might take offense and think you will no longer invest in the child's learning in the same way as you may with another A student. Instead, it can be valuable to provide both some commendation of the B grade along with explaining what the student could have done to achieve a better mark.

The breakdown of confidence and trust in the teacher-parent relationship here is necessary to consider, particularly because parents from certain ethnic backgrounds are nonconfrontational. For example, Middle Eastern parents, specifically mothers, tend to be nonconfrontational out of politeness, even when they disagree with what a teacher is saying. This means they will walk away from the encounter having lost trust that the teacher can provide adequate academic support to their child. As a result of the miscommunication, they might feel the need to hire a private tutor or switch their student to a private school, even if this might not be necessary. Useful strategies to prevent this loss of confidence include making references to work with other students and families from similar backgrounds, to show acceptance within a trusted network, as well as demonstrating a warm and caring approach toward the family, thereby breaking down implied barriers.

An overly warm approach gushing about their child's sense of humor or other traits may fall short with many Chinese families and others, who instead may respond favorably to words like "practical" and "efficient" when talking about their child's work in the class and may put as a priority the student's grades. Along the same lines, if you use the word "efficient" to a Korean parent, they may feel like you, as the teacher, are taking shortcuts and not making their child work hard enough. For this reason, using phrasing like "work ethic" and "hard work," and emphasizing the amount of time their child spent on the work likely will elicit a better reaction and help them fully understand their child is doing well.

Latin American culture at large is warm and personal, so building a relationship with Latin American parents based on those qualities can help create an effective teacher-parent partnership that will lead to student academic success. Being warm and personal also lets them know both they and their child are welcome in the classroom. You might express that the classroom is a "family," and every student is taught to "respect" the teacher and one another.

In Mexican communities, there is a particular word that means "a short person," *chaparro/chaparrito* (male) and *chaparra/chaparrita* (female). It's a familiar term of endearment. One teacher found it helpful in her decades of teaching mainly Mexican and Latin American students and having conversations with their parents to use this term to refer to herself, as a way to create a light-hearted and approachable tone.

When speaking to a typical Mexican parent about their child's work and behavior in school, using words like "obedient" and "well-mannered" are excellent choices, as they will emphasize the respect their child is showing toward you, the teacher. Using a word like "obedient" with many Dominican parents may also foster a trusting parent-teacher relationship. Furthermore, the protective nature of many Dominican parents over their children means that emphasizing that your classroom is a "safe space" for them could go a long way in building trust. Conversely, if you demonstrate too high a focus on the student's objective academic performance, you may be considered as uncaring and cold by some Latin American parents.

Thinking about the difference between some Latin American parents and Slavic parents provides another clear window of understanding into recognizing the way different words and behaviors can impact a teacher's relationship with a parent. Where some Latin American parents may welcome a warm and personal approach to conversation, to some Slavic parents, who value privacy and formality, this approach would likely be off-putting. Calling their child a member of the classroom "family" could be detrimental in some cases, or at least inappropriate and odd. Instead, the use of more formal words to reference academic progress, such as "performance," "accomplishment," and "achievement," has a higher chance of connecting with some Slavic parents than less formal words and phrasing, such as "Your child does good work."

Similar to Latin American culture, Filipino culture also often puts obedience and respect in high regard when it comes to their child's behavior. Therefore, using these words directly can benefit the teacher-parent relationship here. Furthermore, because of the value of family in Filipino culture, small changes in phrasing can have an enormous impact. Instead of saying to a parent, "You should be proud of your child's excellent work," you can rephrase that to, "Your *family* should be proud of your child's excellent work." This use of the word "family" when referencing a student's work can extend to other cultures with deep family ties, such as Korean and Latin American cultures.

In many cultures, the gender of a student impacts the pressure their parents place on them to succeed. Male children are often the ones who usually take the brunt of this pressure in Korean, Indian, Chinese, and Middle Eastern cultures in particular, though certainly it is not limited to them only. In these cultures, the male patriarchal role in the family remains despite living in the United States, where that mindset to a degree may be outdated in many parts of the country. Therefore, thoughtful word choice when talking to parents about a male student becomes even more essential. To connect with traditionally minded families, educators can do well to approach family conversations regarding male students with the mindset that the success of the student is paramount for the identity of the family.

It's important to note again that the attributes and values described are not ones that should be used to describe every family of a particular culture. To reiterate, each of us may be influenced by the culture we grew up in and we've been exposed to in different ways.

Another important note is that when in doubt, just be kind and considerate. Despite the possibilities of distrust and frustration that could form, overall parents know how hard you work and will be able to adjust. They can have the ability to be flexible to adapt to situations, even if the situations are not a cultural norm for them. In fact, for some parents, especially the ones who speak English fluently and pride themselves on it and their ability to adjust to multinational cultures, speaking more slowly or acting differently to them compared to their peers may also feel like an insult.

SUMMARY

When teachers understand the nuance of words in the context of communicating with multicultural parents, interactions will be more controlled and fulfilling. Once confidence or trust between a teacher and a parent is broken, communicating becomes difficult and can get in the way of a student's achievement in the class.

It is important to take the time to research the cultural backgrounds and mindsets of different ethnicities, without typecasting them, as fostering productive relationships between teachers and parents helps to ensure student success. In many ways, this begins with language.

Choosing the correct words in a given conversation can serve as a cue to help parents from different ethnic backgrounds better understand how their child is doing in the class.

SELF-PRACTICE EXERCISES FOR EDUCATORS

CULTURAL DEEP-DIVE

Consider the students on your current roster. Make a list of those who come from multicultural backgrounds. For each ethnicity, do your own research into their background. Understanding their history can provide a lot of insight into their culture. Furthermore, do specific research into parent-child relationships in that culture. For example, if you have first (or even second) generation Korean, Salvadorean, and Somalian students in your class, you will be researching all three of those cultures.

When you finish your research, make yourself a quiz, noting the correct answers. Ideally, you will make it on an app, so you can take the quiz easily, again and again, to reinforce what you learned. Quiz questions should pertain to language to teach yourself not only the words you should use to communicate effectively with those students' parents but also why those words are the best choices. The ultimate goal here is to understand the cultural backgrounds of these parents well enough to be able to communicate with them both effectively and naturally.

INTERACTIVE RESEARCH

Use social media to connect with a person from a different culture and have a conversation.

- Direct messaging, ask questions to inform your perspective, which can, in turn, improve your communication skills.
- Or opt to post on digital forums like Reddit and Quora, asking questions geared at parents of particular ethnicities.

PROMOTING EFFECTIVE CONVERSATIONS

1. Think of a time when you felt your communication with a parent of a different ethnic background was unsuccessful.
   (a) What made it unsuccessful?
   (b) How can understanding the impact of language in these conversations help improve the outcome of these conversations in the future?

(c) Did you feel something you said offended them?

(d) Do you remember using words that might have caused them to lose confidence in you as a teacher?

(e) Do you generally have a standard method of communicating with parents that doesn't consider their cultural background?

2. Put yourself in the shoes of immigrant parents in the United States by imagining yourself as an immigrant parent in another country.

(a) What are some of your cultural norms those teachers need to consider to communicate with you effectively and productively?

(b) What are some examples of words they might choose to bolster the effectiveness of the conversations as they discuss your child's progress with you?

(c) What are your values as a person and (perhaps hypothetically) as a parent?

(d) What language or behavior might you find offensive or off-putting from a teacher?

(e) Why do you think certain words would trigger different responses from you, considering your background and culture?

3. Have students or parents define what the words "good" and "respect" mean to them, as in being a good student, a good parent, respecting your parents, elders, or teachers. What do these words look like?

NOTES

1. Goddard, R, Salloum, S, and Berebitsky, D. Trust as a mediator of the relationships between poverty, racial composition, and academic achievement: evidence from Michigan's public elementary schools. *Educational Administration Quarterly* 45 (2): 292–311.

2. Roan, L., Strong, B., Foss, P. et al. (2009). Social Perspective Taking. U.S. Army Research Institute for the Behavioral and Social Sciences Tech. Rep. 1259.

3. Budiman, A. (2020). Key findings about U.S. immigrants. Pew Research Center. https://www.pewresearch .org/fact-tank/2020/08/20/key-findings-about-u-s-immigrants/ (accessed 19 September 2022).

4. PBS. Global Connections: The Middle East. https://www.pbs.org/wgbh/globalconnections/mideast/ themes/culture/index.html (accessed 19 September 2022).

5. Nisbett, R. and Masuda, T. (2003). Culture and point of view. *Proceedings of the National Academy of Sciences* 100 (19): 11163–11170.

6. Badrinathan, S., Kapur, D., Kay, J., and Vaishnav, M. (2021). Social realities of Indian Americans: results from the 2020 Indian American Attitudes Survey. https://carnegieendowment.org/2021/06/09/social-realities-of-indian-americans-results-from-2020-indian-american-attitudes-survey-pub-84667 (accessed 20 September 2022).

7. Raghavan, P. (2015). Indian parents have very high expectations about their children's education and careers. *Times of India* (18 July). https://timesofindia.indiatimes.com/blogs/minorityview/indian-parents-have-very-high-expectations-about-their-childrens-education-and-careers.

8. David, E. J. (2010). Cultural mistrust and mental health help-seeking attitudes among Filipino Americans. *Asian American Journal of Psychology* 1 (1): 57–66. doi: 10.1037/a0018814.

9. Nadal, K.L. (2011). *Filipino American Psychology: A Handbook of Theory, Research, and Clinical Practice.* Hoboken, NJ: Wiley.

10. Cimmarusti, R.A. (1996). Exploring aspects of Filipino-American families. *Journal of Marital and Family Therapy* 22 (2): 205–217. doi: 10.1111/j.17520606.1996.tb00199.x.

11. Ocampo, A.C. (2013). Am I really Asian?: educational experiences and panethnic identification among second-generation Filipino Americans. *Journal of Asian American Studies* 16 (3) 295–324. doi: 10.1353/jaas.2013.0032.

5

Effective Cross-Cultural Communications in School Contexts

As the world becomes increasingly globalized, cross-cultural interactions between people have increased exponentially. This can be attributed to many reasons, including but not limited to mass immigration, international tourism, and business transactions. Ultimately, this increase in globalization requires all people to pursue a better understanding of effective communications in cross-cultural settings. This process is particularly true for educators, as the personal nature of interactions regarding children requires empathy, understanding, and respect.

This chapter looks at ways that educators can improve their communications with families coming from cross-cultural backgrounds. The more diverse the United States becomes racially and ethnically, the more important it is for educators to learn to manage differences and serve as connectors for their communities.

COMMUNICATION CATEGORIES

Communication can be classified into the following categories

Verbal

The most fundamental type of communication, the spoken word remains as the primary method for imparting messages. As every nation, culture, and ethnicity has their own languages, dialects, and even accents, verbal communication forms are the initial focal point for most cross-cultural interactions.

Nonverbal

Nonverbal communication is an exchange of information through gestures, expressions, and other forms of nonlinguistic cues. Cultural differences can also affect how you use your body language while communicating with others. Nonverbal communication can be a large source of confusion, and cross-cultural offense occurs. For example, in traditional Japanese culture, business cards are expected to be received with a high degree of formality. If an educator takes a card proffered by a parent with a single hand, and puts in a pocket or bag, that parent will take great offense. Even though unspoken, this nonverbal form of communication can be highly charged.

Written

Written communication are all messages conveyed through letters, emails, texts, and other forms of documents. A degree of caution is necessary for educators when writing to recipients from other cultures because the level of formality or informality to use can differ across cultures.

Visual

Visual communication involves sending a message through graphic means such as drawings, graphs, and other illustrations. The main goal of visual communication is to help convey ideas more clearly than through words alone. While using visual methods of communication, in general, can appear impractical since it takes time and effort to produce a suitable illustration to help convey a message, the use of visual methods can help bridge cross-cultural gaps by providing alternative means of expression.

The increasing use of emojis in informal written communications can be a way to gently ensure the intended tone is conveyed. In many Asian social media accounts, cutesier emojis are usually found and expected, even professionally—from hearts to bunnies hugging lovingly, which are not as common in many other cultures, and, in fact, may be considered unprofessional.

The same emoji can be interpreted differently depending on the culture: A waving hand for example could be a sign to break up a friendship in China compared to the Western meaning of "goodbye," and in Pakistan as insults. In many East Asian cultures, more value was placed on emotions showed in the eyes, while Westerners determined emotions based on the appearance of the mouth. For example, to show happiness in Korean or Chinese texts might be ^^ while Americans use :). But the Chinese would see :) as implying distrust or disbelief. Sadness could be TT to Koreans, whereas Americans may use :(. This reflects the tendency of many Koreans to interpret real emotions through the eyes, as they are more difficult to control than the mouth, as compared to Americans and others who interpret emotions based on the mouth, what they consider as the most expressive part of the face. Though complex and not necessarily reflective of low-context/high-context or collectivist/individualistic cultures, in general, more individualistic low-context cultures placed value on self-expression with more emphasis on the mouth. Today, there are even emoji translator jobs because of how culturally specific some emojis have become.

THE ACCULTURATION PROCESS

Part of communicating effectively with people from other cultures is understanding the acculturation process. This process describes the transition of immigrants who move to a new country and how they adapt to their new environment.

This process is similar to assimilation, but it does not have the same connotation because acculturation allows for preserving one's native language, culture, and values. Being "fully assimilated" implies a certain acceptance of the underlying values of the host culture, to the point in which the original attitudes may no longer carry the same weight for decision-making.

A "fully acculturated" individual, meanwhile, understands the expected behaviors within the host culture, but does not necessarily accept them as the "norm" action. That said, the acculturation process is not a decision that immigrants necessarily make on their own; they are influenced by gender, age, and how much interaction they have with the dominant culture.

When different cultural groups come together, there is often an initial adjustment period. This period is called the "culture shock phase" because one might feel different feelings such as disorientation, anxiety, or depression after leaving their familiar environment. If parents (or students) appear to still be in the culture shock phase, it can be important for educators to slow down the pace of the conversation. During this phase, it is important to take things slow and respect where individuals are in adjusting to their new home. This requires patience and understanding from both sides so it can be a positive experience for all parties.

For example, if a parent expresses discomfort in having a conversation in English, it can be important for the educator to demonstrate that this is perfectly okay. Moving to nonverbal communication cues and behaviors to engage the individual can be critical. This is an important time to tailor approaches to the family's culture. For an educator attempting to connect with a shy Korean parent, the steps can be as simple as pouring a cup of tea and inviting them for a guided tour of the school, which in Mexico would mimic giving a tour around the house, an important practice in many Latin American cultures; if trying to build a relationship with a seemingly overwhelmed Colombian parent, sharing photos of the educator's own family may be the best way to make a connection, as examples but not limiting it to these cultures.

It is common for people to feel isolated during this time because they might lack the social support they had in their home country. Educators who creatively find a way to build rapport and draw parents out gently over time can develop a unique relationship that is immensely beneficial to supporting students. Once individuals better understand the people and culture surrounding them in their new country, often they will become more relaxed. This is referred to as the trusting phase because the immigrant feels a sense of security knowing that resources are available to help with any concerns. Parents in this phase can be recognized by their demonstrated knowledge of "how the school works," often due to having an older sibling who has already passed through the system.

Educators should strive to maintain consistency in processes and systems so families who have reached this level of acculturation can feel confident and empowered. Educators working with parents who have passed through to a trusting phase can make use of their unique position to serve as liaisons for more newly arrived parents, helping to address unspoken needs. It is important to note that the length of and degree of each phase is different among individuals; an immigrant family who has lived in the same country for 25 years should assume they are somehow more acculturated than the family who has been in the country for 2 years. Also, there could be some parents who seem culturally and linguistically fluent but actually may not understand even the most common expectations of a student in a classroom, such as participating often. Regardless of the phase or degrees of the phase, it is important to build relationships with individuals undergoing acculturation by creating an environment where they can freely express how they feel and what kind of support would benefit them most.

ADVICE FOR EDUCATORS

The following sections provide brief advice for educators when preparing for and meeting with parents from cultural backgrounds that are different from their own.

GREETINGS

In cross-cultural contexts, you'll need to consider several aspects when conducting initial greetings with someone from a different culture. Aspects such as nationality, age, race, gender, social status, and religion are just some examples that might affect the way you conduct yourself while first meeting families. (See Appendix 2.)

Different countries have different customs regarding ways of greeting other people. For example, in the United States, a person leans toward another individual for a handshake, whereas a bow signifies respect in Japanese and Korean cultures. In many Middle Eastern cultures, meanwhile, contact between a man and woman is forbidden, making a handshake verboten.

For school-based educators, it is not necessary to be perfect in your cross-cultural greetings. However, understanding the background of your families and demonstrating an effort to make an initial gesture fitting with cultural norms can lay the foundation for positive interactions moving forward.

AVOID SLANG, JARGON, METAPHORS

Slang, jargon, and metaphors are not always easily understood, so they need to be avoided in cross-cultural communication contexts. For example, if you want to say a student is behaving inappropriately, using the slang "has a chip on his shoulder" creates an initial distance between the educator and the family, and changes the focus of the conversation from the onset. Educators need to make sure words are chosen carefully and precisely to avoid potential issues.

STARTING WITH A SMILE?

Smiles are an important nonverbal form of communication. They help us express happiness, sadness, irony, or confusion. However, they are not always easy to read by people from different cultures. As previously mentioned, many people from Slavic and Nordic backgrounds can view smiles with a degree of distrust, and an overly smiling educator may be perceived as less trustworthy in general.

Even with cultures where smiling is more commonly acceptable, educators should be aware that a "polite smile" from a quiet parent can mask much confusion.

BRAIN RESPONSES TO NONVERBAL SIGNALS

The brain has a natural tendency to respond differently to nonverbal forms of communication, such as gestures and body language.

Our brain tends to respond favorably to patterns, and it likes familiarity, so if the faculty and staff all come from the same country or have similar customs, it makes communicating with them much easier. However, people from other cultures might not understand these signals because they originate from different cultures, so you need to be careful when using them.

For example, in the United States, shrugging your shoulders can be used to communicate uncertainty about something. However, many people from other cultures can feel insulted when someone shrugs their shoulders as it is perceived as a sign of disrespect. For example, many Latin Americans expect educators to display a degree of emotion and personal care when discussing their child's performance; if the educator's body language instead depicts nonchalance, this can be taken as a sign of unprofessionalism.

Retraining your brain and body to adapt to other forms of communication is an important skill to learn if you want to effectively communicate in a cross-cultural context. It can help you develop or abandon habits that are not always effective when communicating with someone from a different culture.

How Do Other Cultures Best Receive Communication?

Understanding the ways in which communications are received in another culture is important if you want to communicate effectively. Finding the best possible way to communicate can be tricky. If the preferred method is difficult to ascertain, then a period of observation can be helpful. This is often best achieved by watching how students interact with their parents and how the parents interact with each other. Once you get a good grasp on how the parents prefer to communicate, you'll be able to send them information in a way that they understand and respect.

The bottom line is that respecting and being sensitive to the needs of all cultures involved in cross-cultural communication is not always easy because significant differences often can lead to miscommunication. However, it's doable with the right mindset and preparation.

Variable Praise Comfort Levels

One obstacle that can make it difficult to communicate effectively with people from different cultures is respecting their preferences for positive reinforcement, the response to which can vary. Not everyone responds best to outright praise, so try other methods such as showing appreciation through a gesture or giving them a responsibility that allows them to feel more valued within the organization. In Japan, unless coming from a superior to an inferior, compliments can carry a connotation as being mildly passive-aggressive.

TRAINING INTERNATIONAL AND NON-FOREIGN BORN EDUCATORS

Ongoing training and education on school values and behavior for international and non-foreign born faculty and staff will help reduce the risk of slipups due to cultural confusion.

It is also important to make sure all educators are familiar with each other's cultures at work. This way, people from different countries will understand how best to interact with one another and what type of support to give. The earlier educators are educated, the closer they may feel to their fellow teachers and the school as a whole. Even if the school doesn't offer formal cross-cultural training, it is a good idea to seek out advice from those colleagues with personal experience in other cultures. The more support provided for everyone, the easier it will be to get through any potential difficulties and provide greater tools to talk with parents more effectively.

SUMMARY

Communicating with those from different backgrounds takes time and patience. It is natural for educators (like many people) to feel awkward when interacting with families with whom they do not share the same cultural background. However, building effective means of communication with families from diverse cultural backgrounds will bring fresh ideas and perspectives to our teaching practice, ultimately benefiting students.

SELF-REFLECTIVE EXERCISES FOR EDUCATORS

1. If you are studying in a new country and do not speak the language fluently, consider how you might convey each of the following through verbal, nonverbal, written, and visual communication methods:

    ◦ Being late.

    ◦ Asking for clarification on a homework assignment.

    ◦ Treating your teacher with respect.

    ◦ What questions come up for you, the responses to which could help you effectively communicate? What would you want your teacher to know about you?

2. Choose an ethnic, cultural, or national background that is well represented in your school's demographics. Think about potential strategies for talking to parents who are still in the "culture shock phase" of acculturation. How would you help them feel comfortable?

PART II

THE FAMILY AND THE CLASSROOM

6

PERSPECTIVES ON THE EDUCATOR'S ROLE

The educator's role has many facets, all of which are crucial in establishing a modern, functional learning environment. Understanding how cultural differences can impact the perception of what a learning environment should be is crucial in this era of global collaboration, as assumptions about student knowledge of how the school "works" can lead to wasted productivity and damaged attitudes. This chapter begins the process of looking into cross-cultural differences around perspectives on the roles of educators, parents, and students, and how they impact classroom practices.

FAULTY BEGINNINGS, FAULTY ENDS

Imagine that you are a mechanic, and today is your first day on your job. You know your role is to fix cars, but you probably don't know how to check in clients, where your tools are, how much time is allocated for each task, and so forth. You arrive to work at 8:00 a.m. and your new boss orders you to your workstation with no direction, assuming you already know the basics. You look around and make a guess at which car seems to need work, replacing a broken carburetor with materials that you find.

Fast-forward four to six months later. You have picked up on some essential routines and probably located a few tools, but no one has taught you the "in-house" rules of the game. Your workdays are not as productive as they're supposed to be half a year into your job.

Now not only are your workdays less productive, but your attitude is taking a turn because you are frustrated.

Unfortunately, this is often how many students and families from international backgrounds are set up at the start of each academic year. On the first day of school, learners arrive in an exciting environment, knowing their goal is to learn and grow via educational experience. They also develop expectations about practices and behaviors that educators or instructors should exhibit during the learning process and their classroom obligations. These obligations include preparing assignments for class, class participation, the appropriateness of questioning the educator in class, and more.

For students coming from multicultural backgrounds, these obligations are assumed to be "already known," as well-intentioned educators can fail or don't have the time to recognize that particular students are new to the ways in which school systems and classrooms work in the U.S. context. Educators have the power to impact the lives of their students. Making use of an inclusive, thoughtful teaching approach and creating a culturally inclusive learning environment can have a positive impact on the learners far beyond the classroom.

CLASSROOM EXPECTATIONS

Guidelines, both implicit and explicit, exist in every classroom to help teachers and students understand the behaviors expected throughout the school day. They allow teachers to focus on academic instruction and imparting lesson material. A classroom without consistent expectations lacks the necessary structure students need to be successful. Reliable guidelines allow educators to anticipate student behavior, making it possible to plan for expected barriers and focus on the students' academic needs. They also provide students a road map of what they are to do and how they are to participate. Such clear structure will make it easier to talk with parents about a child's performance and expectations.

Without clearly defined classroom expectations, students are often left to figure out for themselves what's considered "acceptable" behavior. Like the mechanic choosing which car to work on, students make their best guess about what to do during study halls and other unstructured times. This takes time and is learned through trial and error, potentially resulting in lost productivity. Establishing classroom expectations early on and reviewing them regularly gives educators and learners the chance to devote more time to teaching and learning.

Realistic classroom expectations should be:

- Created to meet the specific needs of each classroom (for educators and students).

- Individualized to each class but generalized for all students in that class.

- Stated positively and clearly.
- Well-defined, achievable, and support positive learning experiences.

Creating the correct classroom expectations gives educators a set of observable behaviors to reinforce. It's important that these expectations are stated clearly and taught to learners to prevent ambiguity. Similarly, the content of classroom expectations must be consistent with the academic and behavioral goals of the learning institution.

Examples of common behavior expectations in the classroom include:

- Raising a quiet hand.
- Keeping feet and hands to self.
- Using appropriate language.

Examples of common academic expectations in the classroom include:

- Tracking content with a finger.
- Making the necessary correction as you go.
- Answering questions on signal.

TEACHERS' EXPECTATIONS OF PARENTS

The parent-teacher relationship is an essential aspect of students' success. The beginning of a new school year creates the opportunity for educators or teachers to set the tone for establishing strong teacher-parent relationships.

Teachers expect parents to support them in various ways, which include:

- Helping educators to better understand the students.
- Sharing a goal of clarity, consistency, and fairness in all parent-teacher interactions.
- Treating teachers with respect.
- Conveying respect for teachers' authority.
- Not criticizing teachers in students' presence, if at all.
- Appreciating the demands and constraints of the educator's job.
- Helping teachers monitor the child's schoolwork.

- Supporting teachers whenever they take an appropriate disciplinary action.
- Keeping the teacher informed of family-related events with direct impact on the child's school activities and performance.

As an educator, working with parents is a two-way street. Let them know what you expect, as this may help establish a strong relationship that will benefit your students in many ways.

PARENTS' EXPECTATIONS OF TEACHERS

Most parents and families have assumptions around the roles of an educator and the expected outcomes of the students in terms of behavior, academic assessments, character development, and more. These assumptions may be determined by their personal cultural norms. Therefore, it's essential for teachers to clearly define what parents should expect as this will help align the interests and expectations of parents with what happens in a classroom. As the professional in charge of children in school, it's crucial to clarify what parents should expect from educators regarding the following, keeping in mind that many parents, especially those used to more authoritative roles of teachers, would not be familiar with them or think that it's their place to have an opinion:

- Student engagement.
- Fairness and equal learning opportunities for students, especially their own.
- The cycle of teaching and learning (including communication of classroom goals, student engagement, corrective feedback, formative assessment, cooperative learning, and more).

Effectively defining what is expected of teachers eliminates confusion and misunderstandings and makes it easy for parents and other school stakeholders to hold educators accountable. Otherwise, teacher expectations are likely to be a list of statements on a piece of paper instead of well-thought-out actions that could lead to desired results.

The primary goal of a classroom should be to optimize student success through behavioral and academic achievement. This can only be done by instituting reliable and consistent classroom routines and expectations. As many teachers already know, building strong classroom management supports long-term student success and alleviates stressors such as common behavioral concerns. Helping every "new mechanic" to know which car they are supposed to work on first ultimately helps educators focus on teaching and students focus on learning.

CULTURAL VIEW OF THE TEACHER

As an educator, you probably have experienced this situation: an individual asks about your profession. You tell them you are a teacher, and they sometimes show a strong reaction one way or the other. For instance, some people will gasp and perhaps tell you how brave you are, while others will tell you they think you're severely underpaid. Still others will talk about how overpaid you are because you have summers off and how nice it is to work in a school.

Either way, nearly everyone has an opinion on the role of educators and the teaching profession. These opinions and perceptions vary depending on culture and other factors. For instance, education is perceived as an essential foundation of success in many countries globally. Therefore, teachers are held in high regard. In some regions, educators are perceived as being more than simple professionals who pass knowledge to students but as default "problem-solvers" for all aspects of life.

This is not uncommon in countries where teachers are viewed as a partner in holistic child development. Marina was teaching an eighth-grade student in English literature earlier in her career. This student was ethnically Korean, but identified strongly as an American, as she had lived in the United States since fifth grade. Her mother, however, adhered more closely to her native Korean culture, as she found the U.S. culture confusing to her. One day, the student's mother handed Marina a biology book and asked if she could teach her child about the reproductive system and pregnancy—the birds and the bees. For this parent, after having established a strong trust, the role of an educator extended well beyond the particular curriculum into any area in which support was needed. That teacher is a part of the village, calling back to the village metaphor, and responsibilities are fluid.

The parent wasn't really asking to teach the eighth grader biology. She was asking her to talk about sex education and abstinence in American culture, something she was not culturally fluent to do. To deny this request meant Marina would be extracting herself from the village and surely a distance would form. The mother would never say why but it would be clear that her loyalty and respect to Marina would wane. Marina warmly obliged. It wasn't the effectiveness of the lesson itself that was important, but that Marina, through this action, was telling the mother that Marina was still a part of the village.

HOLISTIC CHILD DEVELOPMENT CAN BECOME THE NORM

As seen in the previous example, parents from international backgrounds can place great trust in those in the role of the educator. A holistic approach to child development pays attention to the child's physical, personal, social, spiritual, and emotional well-being and various cognitive aspects of learning. A student's learning can be perceived as integrated and interconnected, even when a teacher plans or assesses with a focus on a specific outcome or component of the learning process. Therefore, educators should recognize the connections between children, communities, and families and the significance of reciprocal relationships for learning.

For many educators, a holistic approach involves recognizing and identifying, teaching, supporting, counseling, encouraging, challenging, and including children in their development. It encourages children to explore all their capacities and intelligence to discover the world in all its wholeness. For example, Finland adopted phenomenon-based learning, a holistic learning approach that shifts focus from the individual subject to topics and phenomena such as technology, water, and media. This interdisciplinary approach facilitates constructivist and inquiry-based teaching techniques that redefine the role of an educator from "sage-on-the-stage" to "guide-on-the-side."

Understanding this role can help in the communication with the parents. This does not mean teachers need to change their entire curriculum or the approach to a set curriculum, although certainly these expectations can inspire teachers to be better and better, as one had said earlier. Teachers can emphasize certain points of their curriculum or approach during interactions with the parents. For more grades-oriented parents, where they may be thinking "How is this going to get my kid into a 'good' college?," mentioning the grades or how this approach could lead to stronger grades would be more effective.

IT'S NOT ALL UP TO THE KIDS

Individual responsibility is the belief that people choose and control their actions and destiny. It is generally accepted in U.S. educational contexts that your actions are your responsibility and you should be legally and morally responsible for the consequence of your actions.

Although this is a legally and psychologically murky area that lacks a precise definition, the idea of individual responsibility is commonly accepted. However, the influence of past experiences and general upbringing on others cannot be overstated. For this reason, students may not always be fully responsible for their choices and actions. When it comes to students' choices regarding their education, some cultures place more responsibility on educators to serve as a primary decision maker.

Educators are, therefore, recommended to discuss the level of personal agency and accountability parents wish their children to have. Do your students often give excuses for their poor performance? Do you often get excuses like "the questions were too challenging" or "there was not enough time to prepare" from your students? If so, student accountability is an excellent trait to develop in learners as it helps them take responsibility for their learning and actions, as well as improving their academic performance and achievements.

Given the developmental stage of the prefrontal cortex for risk and responsibility in adolescent brains, some students may not understand the importance of taking responsibility for their actions. This is why it's crucial that educators frame rules at the start of the years on acceptable and nonacceptable actions in the classroom. Inappropriate or unacceptable behavior must have well-defined and understood consequences and be monitored closely. The students will then decide whether they choose to act appropriately or inappropriately. For example, a student who understands that the consequence of misbehaving in the classroom is detention will calibrate his behavior accordingly. Understanding this concept will help students be responsible for their actions. Sharing clear expectations with the parents could prevent later confusion. These rules must be firm because leniency encourages children to break the rules. When an educator bends the rules for a student, others will expect similar treatment, and parents who communicate with other parents in the school may start to give pushback. Generally, parents who understand the more holistic teaching style, where educators teach students individual responsibility and accountability, though with some parents not at the sacrifice of grades, may help the parents to develop more trust in the teachers.

WHO'S ACCOUNTABLE?

In most Western countries, there is a high sense of individual responsibility placed on children. The husband of one of Marina's colleagues, who would identify as "White American," had parents who let him choose in second grade whether or not he wanted to skip a grade. His teacher said he was well beyond the level of other students in his grade. He chose not to skip the grade because he was afraid of needing to make new friends. While remaining in the second grade, he quickly became bored by the relatively easy workload, and began to misbehave frequently. In this case, his parents believed that they were providing him with the right level of agency, and thus held him accountable for his subsequent misbehaviors in class.

In many East Asian cultures and others, the parents would find that it's the teacher's role to inform parents to skip the grade or not. A common saying in multiple languages is a respectfully toned form of, "You're the teacher. You would know. I defer to you."

The parents from these cultures would expect input and tangible guidance from educators, which would be considered with a much higher priority than the expressed desires of the student. If the teachers don't express an expert opinion, the parents may think that the teacher is lazy, doesn't care about their children, doesn't know how to give guidance (and, therefore, are not good at their jobs), and is not in tune with the students' needs.

From our professional experience, the level of agency children are expected to have may be among the areas with the highest variability across cultures. For example, when conducting a college consulting session with Marie, a parent from a traditional New England culture, it was clear that most academic decisions where up to her daughter, Joan. Marie was extremely comfortable leaving decisions about classes in high school up to Joan, saying, "I'm not sure if this may feel like too much for Joan once school starts—but I'm going to leave it in her hands. If she wants to adjust, she should work through that herself. She knows she has your guidance when she wants it/needs it."

In a similar conversation with a traditional Indian family, the student, Albert, talked about where he might like to pursue university studies, sharing his love of Denmark. Albert had widely traveled in the country, and very much enjoyed the food and the social environment. Albert had very little personal incentive to study in the United States or Canada and didn't include any colleges there on his initial lists. Albert's mother, meanwhile, decided that Albert must study in either the United States or Canada, due to her perception of better employment prospects. Albert's own preferences were not seen as relevant to the decision-making.

Within every learning environment, there's a prevailing culture that influences other aspects of classroom activities. The choice of content, attitudes and skills promoted, teacher-student relationships, and other aspects of the learning environment are deeply influenced by culture. This is the main reason parents tend to place their children in learning institutions that reflect their beliefs and values and that they believe will give their children the right kind of advantages, even if it means at the cost of losing their language.

This cultural match starts in even preschool where a school may have adapted a more child-centered/play-based model. Some families may not as readily grasp the concept so the students may come overdressed, and they expect the toddler to stay neat and clean, contrary to the American progressive model of getting muddy is good. Some families might still be spoon-feeding their child, which can turn off some teachers and other parents. Calling back to the collectivist/individualist cultures, there could be a judgment made against the parent for not encouraging the child to feed herself independently. It's important for teachers not to assume and not judge, as you may not know the cultural context. However, whose role is it to support families in understanding a new set of values sometimes important to their survival?

Some parents unfortunately will need to find out on their own the hard way. For example, during a high school tour where a bilingual educator accompanied a Korean parent for the week, she noticed the mother brought over one large suitcase that contained her son's canned or instant pack versions of his favorite meals. "Bob" was the only male child and was given all the resources the family could provide. She had Bob eat first and sometimes spoon-fed him to eat another bite of a certain dish. The educator, concerned the parent had no idea about the appropriate behavior within the American context, mentioned how such behavior can be seen as "babying" and would be looked down on. After a few more repeated attempts with no change in behavior, the educator realized it didn't matter what she said.

A few years later, the mother reached out again. The educator was told that Bob had been accepted to a highly selective school, a perfect academic match for the family. To them, as it is to some families, a perfect match meant a name-brand match. One wintery day during Bob's junior year, his American roommate, whom he wasn't on the best of terms with, saw his mother buttoning up Bob's coat, not an uncommon if not typical practice. His roommate told other students and the teen, unfortunately, was bullied, and with the pressures of junior year and the stress of getting into one of the most highly selective universities, Bob developed a mental health issue and was put on leave for two semesters. The mother realized then that she was indeed "babying" him, so much so that he didn't develop the independence, resilience, and grit he needed to navigate society.

Thus, even if there is what seems to be a school match in the parents' eyes, it's important to understand why they think it so. It might be that they believe a match in culture of a school means a match in academic strength, reputation, and prestige. This may not be the best place for the child and family, and as much as educators can do to support the families, it is always going to be their decision.

Still, we can still explore and implement the right education program. In the case above, the educator might have tried a more nuanced approach that gave Bob's parents ways to honor their sense of role without overtly "babying" him. If this behavioral pattern held true for many families in the classroom, this may have been the necessary impetus to create curriculum that equipped the students and parents to discuss actively how their actions expressed different emotions. Ultimately, such a supportive learning environment fosters a wider appreciation of human differences and enables all stakeholders to prosper.

CULTURAL DIVERSITY IN THE CLASSROOM

American classrooms have become more culturally diverse, which means cultural diversity is an increasingly important issue for educators. This is why educators should embrace diversity and foster culturally inclusive classrooms designed to help students succeed. Culture is more than a list of food preferences, holidays, or the language people speak. It is the framework around which one's identity is built. It influences how you engage with the world, the expectations you have, and the perspectives you take. Everyone has a culture, and most Americans have identities built from different cultures.

Educators must ensure they don't neglect any aspects of students' culture, much harder to do when certain aspects of a culture—beliefs, perceptions, core values, etc.—are largely unseen. This is why it's important to engage with various cultures and seek out cultural training. Also, educators must foster a learning environment where cultural diversity is understood and accepted, particularly when cultural differences have historical significance. As no two students are the same, to foster cultural awareness in the classroom, the educator must understand cultural aspects that can influence students' attitudes, perceptions, and behaviors.

SUMMARY

This chapter addressed the varying conceptions of the roles of educators, students, and parents, and what different expectations might be placed on each other in cross-cultural interactions. Recommendations were given, with the hopeful message that holistic child development can become the norm.

SELF-REFLECTIVE EXERCISES FOR EDUCATORS

- Interview your parents (or other members of your parents' generation). Ask them about their expectations of the role of a student, parent, and teacher. Ask them about what was important to them in a school. What makes sense to you? What (if anything) seems archaic?

- Choose an ethnic, cultural, or national background that is well represented in your school's demographics. Research and watch popular television shows or movies that are popular in the "home country" for that background. Take notes on what they reveal to you about the culture.

7

CULTURAL VALUES AND DIVERSITY

Cultural diversity is what gives our world its richness and beauty. The differences in values that occur in different cultures translate into a wide array of perceptions on what truly matters within the world.

For educators, the ability to anticipate how lesson material and communicative messages need to be altered to suit diversity within the classroom becomes a critical skill. A multicultural audience can present one of the biggest hidden obstacles for communication, as differences in cultural values widen, the gaps between a message's intention and its impact widen with cultural gaps.

This chapter provides an overview on aspects of cultural diversity that can affect classroom dynamics. As educators develop greater cultural sensitivity, they become more likely to acknowledge the possibility of cultural gaps arising in their classroom, and take proactive steps to ensure that all students are effectively supported.

TOUCHING ON TERMINOLOGY

The words "culture," "customs," and "values" are often used interchangeably, but they are all components of a bigger picture.

Essentially, a custom is a tradition that demonstrates a community's cultural values. On the other hand, values run deeper than what is observed on the surface. Values can be understood and put together by observing various customs passed down over several generations. For example, the Korean custom of celebrating an infant's first birthday, known as *doljanchi*, involves an elaborate set of traditional practices, including providing gold rings as gifts and setting out highly symbolic table decorations. The highlight of the celebration is the *doljabi*, a game where items such as books, stethoscopes, coins, or balls are laid out to represent different passions and future careers. The infant "chooses" one of the items while the assembled partygoers cheer, providing a fun and happy memory for all.

The customs involved in the *doljanchi* are indicative of a deep-set cultural value placed on family. This value has its roots in Confucian practices, and was also shaped by the harsh reality of life in Korea before the country developed modern healthcare. In the 1800s, the infant mortality rate in Korea was over 50%. Even in the 1950s, one out of every four children on the Korean peninsula died before reaching their first birthday. This context helped to develop the strong cultural value placed on making sacrifices to ensure the survival and prosperity of children, and led to the custom of celebrating the completion of an infant's first year, even in the most humble households.

Culture can thus be defined as a community's guiding values and beliefs. These values are inculcated through the customary rituals that can be seen throughout a society. Individuals naturally learn cultural values through repeated exposure to traditional customs, strengthening their relationships and ensuring their recognition by other members of the community.

Diversity is often brought up as a value when speaking about multicultural contexts. Diversity goes beyond age and race and refers to a wide range of demographic variables. The common areas of diversity include gender, sexuality, religion, ethnicity, race, nationality, age, education, socioeconomic background, skills, and culture. Cultural diversity is the coexistence of diverse beliefs, art, knowledge, norms, abilities, religion, languages, and customs.

FAMILY DIVERSITY

Every culture has its own definition of what constitutes the "ideal" family, and deviations from that standard are considered dysfunctional according to their distance from the ideal. There are of course a wide range of dimensions and characteristics in which families differ within and across cultures, and different family groupings can function effectively. Family diversity can be seen as the variations that exist along demographic and structural dimensions as well as differences in the communicative processes within the family itself.

There are five key elements of family diversity:[1]

1. *Cultural diversity* creates differences in the traditions and lifestyles of families with different religious beliefs and ethnic roots.

2. *Organizational diversity* is the variance in household types, family structures, kinship patterns, and even the division of labor within a household.

3. *Life-cycle diversity* in family diversity is the differences in family life between couples with children and families that don't have children.

4. *Class diversity* as an element of family diversity creates differences in income, for instance, between the middle-income and working-class families.

5. *Cohort diversity* as an element of family diversity comes across as families passing through different stages of the family life cycle.

FAMILY MAKEUP

Immigrant families comprise one or more members who have moved from another country. Some family members may decide to immigrate, come and go, stay in the sending country, or go back to their country temporarily. One major defining feature of the immigrant family is the relatively low level of assimilation to the "new country," particularly among adult generations. These older members of the family are unwilling or unable to let go of their home culture, and thus may be more emphatic about the maintenance of particular customs, rituals, and traditions.

International families, meanwhile, often comprise a child or children and/or one or both parents to be a national of a country other than the one they live in. It could also be a family who is living in a country other than their country of origin. An international family may also include a child who is away from their country of origin or spouses holding assets in a foreign country. International families may also comprise a family residing in their country of origin but having one member located overseas, usually the father, to earn the money to support the child and mother. Some of these families don't have permanent resident or citizenship status, which is what families need to stay long term. Culturally, an international family and an immigrant family from the same country may have different values. There are also, of course, blended cultural families, which comprise couples or children from other ethnic groups with various lifestyles, preferences, and traditions.

CONSIDERING CULTURAL VALUES AND CORE BELIEFS

Culture is the cumulative transfer of experience, beliefs, values, knowledge, religion, and other concepts of the universe across generations, resulting in a system of knowledge about "what should be done" amongst a given group of people. This system is a cumulation of experiences and learnings and is nurtured in younger generations through interactions and patterns of behavior, commonly transmitted by artifacts and symbols. The accepted way of life of a given community or group of people is often illustrative of their cultural values.

CORE BELIEFS AND PRACTICES

These values ultimately result in an implicit "default programming" of the mind, creating a set of deeply held core beliefs about how the world works that frame all interactions and experiences. This "programming" defines values and, therefore, makes members of one cultural community readily distinguishable from other groups of people. In its most readily apparent form, our cultural encoding can be seen through variations in attenuation to stimuli in our environment.

One illustrative example of this came early in Seth's teaching career. A fellow teacher from Thailand pulled him aside one morning with a highly distraught look, noting she had an urgent matter to discuss. Thinking he'd made a major faux pas in his lesson planning or departmental responsibilities, Seth sat down over a coffee, ready to make adjustments. With a very serious expression, the Thai teacher told Seth he needed to make sure he remembered to iron his shirt every day to match the "proper appearance" expected from a teacher in Thai society.

Thus, core beliefs are the deeply held assumptions people have about how things "ought to be" for themselves, others, and the world. These beliefs are often deeply ingrained in their thinking and usually shape their behaviors and reality. Often, the ideas develop from people's childhood and through their experiences with the world around them.

These core beliefs are the roots of a group's behaviors and perceptions of the world, creating the aspects of culture that we see on the surface. Within longstanding and well-defined cultures, core beliefs are formalized into specific societal laws that define what practices are acceptable and what are banned. A group of people's beliefs about certain symbols may also be a part of their culture and used to invoke certain emotions and feelings. A ready (and controversial) example of this are the proscribed regulations around dress codes in conversative Islamic states, placing high penalties on females who do not meet the strict requirements for wearing hijab or other coverings. The difference in underlying core beliefs around these regulations can be witnessed by the innately negative reaction from many Western societies toward such rules.

CATEGORIZING CULTURAL VALUES AND CORE BELIEFS

Much of the foundational research work on cultural values was performed by the Dutch social psychologist Geert Hofstede. Toward the end of the twentieth century, Hofstede conducted comprehensive studies of how values in the workplace are influenced by culture in different nations, defining culture as "the collective programming of the mind." In Hofstede's model,[2] there are six dimensions of national culture.

Power Distance Index

This dimension determines the extent to which the society accepts inequalities and ingrained social hierarchies. The level of the index is determined by the core beliefs of less powerful members; the more who accept and expect that power is distributed unequally, the higher the index. Lower power distance within cultures can manifest in comfort in questioning authority, higher social mobility, and normalized goals for distributing resources equally.

Individualism versus Collectivism Index

This dimension focuses on the strength of the relationship between individuals to the various groups in which they belong. Highly collectivist societies are characterized by strong bonds and high loyalty toward all "in-group" members, while the bonds in more individualized societies may only extend to immediate family members. In societies with lower collectivist preferences, societal good may be given a lower priority than individual freedom of choice.

Uncertainty Avoidance Index

This dimension can be defined as the relative tolerance within a culture for ambiguity and flexibility. Societies with a higher level of uncertainty avoidance tend to be characterized by strict laws and regulations, as well as a general acceptance of the existence of one "absolute truth." A lower degree of uncertainty avoidance can result in societies where regular changes in plans are more accepted, and alterations to governing structures can be expected to occur.

Masculinity versus Femininity Index

Hofstede's nomenclature for this index is open to criticism for the continuance of archaic relations to gender, and it may be more appropriate to consider this as a "competition versus cooperation" index. Regardless, societies with a higher degree of masculinity (as defined by Hofstede) demonstrate higher preferences for material achievement and heroism, while more feminine-oriented societies are characterized by a focus on quality of life and caring for all members of the community.

Long-Term Orientation Index

This dimension focuses on the degree to which the past dictates current and future decision-making and actions. A lower degree on this index can manifest in a higher pattern of honoring traditions and a reluctance to accept changes to societal patterns or organizational structures. Societies with higher levels of long-term orientation, meanwhile, place a strong value on pragmatic problem-solving and regular adaptations to ways of working according to the current situation.

Indulgence versus Restraint Index

This dimension determines the relative amount of freedom related to the gratification of basic needs by individuals in a society. In highly indulgent cultures, communities generally accept rationales of enjoyment and desire fulfillment by individuals for actions that may cross societal norms. In restrained cultures, these societal norms are paramount, and individual enjoyment is given a lower priority.

Hofstede's research is widely used in workplace and academic settings and provides a useful starting place for thinking about variations in cultural values and core beliefs. Different groups demonstrate these cultural dynamics at different degrees of intensity, affected by both long- and short-term contextual influences.

For instance, in some traditional Black communities in the American South, the perpetuation of racist practices during the Jim Crow and Civil Rights eras have given rise to more highly collectivist values, with group membership and loyalties extended beyond the immediate family to religious and other "in-group" members. The need for survival required the development of tighter bonds within these communities, including the powerful relationships created within Baptist church groups. Lacking the same constant threat, White American culture in the New England region of the United States, meanwhile, developed a more highly "masculine" and "heroic" culture, focusing on the accumulation of material possessions, individualism, competition, and mastery of nature.

While variations certainly exist within different groups, it is essential to note that different cultural groups can (and almost always do, as stated in Chapter 4) have some common ground for cultural values and core beliefs. The collective spiritualism within many Southern Black communities echoes the religion-based bonds within Islamic cultures, while the masculine-competition orientation of White New Englanders is matched by a similarly heroic sensibility of many Latin Americans.

FORMATION OF CULTURAL VALUES

It is important to note that culture is not genetically acquired but acquired through language and modeling. Culture is also usually encoded in the semantics and vocabulary of a language. A person acquainted with more than one language is in an excellent position to understand that emotions, norms, and concepts are not available in another. For example, the Korean expression of *jung* relates to a deep-seated emotional bond between people, either family members, friends, or close professional relationships, as well as to animals and even to some sentimental places. This expression does not have an immediate parallel in

English, and understanding that absences of these ideas exist is a key part of developing respect for the presence of alternate ways of living.

Culture is acquired through regular and repeated exposure to a group of people's actions, judgments, and norms. As life is a learning process, many have constant opportunities to learn about our cultures. In the process of learning, people also find themselves adopting elements from cultures different from their own, especially when they have an opportunity to live in different cultural environments.

Cultural values are primarily formed through environmental adaptations, social evolution, and the influence of historical factors. Contact with other groups demonstrating alternative cultural values can have radically different impacts on a community's cultural values, with a counterreaction of strengthening existing norms or a more gradual assimilation of the values of the other group. In this evolutionary process, individuals are able to develop perceptual patterns that determine their reaction to stimuli or judgment of events, people, and objects.

Cultural values and systems are created when individuals in a community gradually learn rules that prioritize specific values. For example, the *jung* concept in Korea may be more tangible for youth when their bond with a childhood friend is given deep respect and priority by older generations. Culture is formed through these subtle processes as newcomers gradually understand the dynamics of their surrounding culture. They develop norms and values necessary and appropriate for survival within the surrounding cultural context, as their actions are directed or limited by the implicit rules within the surrounding community.

ROLE OF CULTURAL VALUES

It is worth noting that cultural diversity is not ethnic diversity. Ethnicity is a social construct, and ethnic groups are individuals who are related to each other by virtue of characteristics such as language, religion, and culture.

Culture can be considered the vein of the society through which life flows. Shared cultural values bind people together and make them united and strong. Culture manifests itself as people's practices, religion, language, lifestyle, and even food. As people learn about a culture and develop an understanding of it, aspects of their characters, perceptions, and personalities are created in the process and inform people on how best to respond to situations. For example, the decisions about prioritizing one's individual desire for what to eat for dinner over the wishes of others in one's family may be governed by the normalized level of indulgence within one's culture.

Being able to acculturate into a culture can be essential as it allows people to become part of a community and exist within it harmoniously. These values give future generations an opportunity to understand ideologies and practices and their importance in guiding their life within a society. Through the transmission and evolution of cultural values, new generations are able to adopt the ideals of their society and practice behaviors that allow them to survive in a community.

WHAT DOES THE EXISTENCE OF CULTURAL GAPS MEAN FOR EDUCATION?

Educators who demonstrate and model respect for the process of learning about cultural values provide space for students to build their self-identity, self-esteem, enhance their resilience, and develop their thinking skills. As educators manage behaviors in the classroom, they must keep in mind the reality of a gap in cultural values and the role it plays in students' behaviors.

While the United States is often considered to be a paragon of multiculturalism, the appropriate behavior, practices, and cultural values often put an emphasis on traditional "White" cultural norms, which then manifest in school policies, behavioral expectations in the learning environments, communication, and even the engagement of family. This default gap can result in disparities in the expectations of diverse students from teachers and the learners' worldview and can negatively impact the success of students from different cultures.

One telling example of this from Marina's experience came from a consultancy with a New England school with a substantial Chinese student population. The school was experiencing what was (in their view) a highly troubling series of episodes of plagiarism and "work-sharing" amongst the Chinese students. Despite numerous punitive measures, the students continued to divide and collaborate on assignments, causing great consternation within the faculty. During the intervention session with the students, Marina worked with the students to understand themselves; eventually, besides understanding the ethical implications separate from the cultural value, the student actions were still related to their core belief of collectivism, and a difference of perception of "individual work" as related to regular school assignments designed for learning. By determining the root cause of the behavior, the school was able to "meet the students where they were" and guide them to better understand some of the more confusing parts of academic honesty that were seen differently.

In a related example, at some universities in Korea, a common expectation for students preparing a research paper a few years ago was to collect as much relevant information on the scope of the topic as possible. The work would show the hard work the students put in to appreciate and respect the opinions of the scholars on the topic. This would not be a common assignment by professors in the United States. Students studying in the United States after having such assignments may have a harder time in writing critical analytical research papers and meeting the expectations of the professors at an American university.

IDENTIFYING CULTURAL GAPS

It is crucial for both educators and learners to acknowledge the possibility of cultural gaps in the classroom. They also need to be aware that there is a likelihood of problems arising. There is a need for both learners and educators to take a more thoughtful approach and for understanding toward culturally diverse students.

Through this, they will ensure students with different backgrounds and needs succeed in the school environment. It also creates a culture of acceptance that allows learners to thrive in the diverse world. Diversity in the classroom will increase constantly, and educators need to prepare the environment for the upcoming dynamics.

Identifying the cultural gaps will aid education institutions and teachers in making the curriculum and the classroom environment attain the cultural diversity of the society we exist in. Learners can then identify strategies like creating cultural awareness in the classroom by understanding individual students, incorporating cultural diversity in the lesson plans, and practicing sensitivity to cultures. This allows them to give culturally diverse learners the freedom and flexibility they need and be responsible educators in doing so. If institutions are actively recruiting international students or appreciate diversity in classrooms, then we must be responsible in identifying the gaps and providing tools and resources for all the stakeholders, the members of the village.

SUMMARY

As great cultural diversity exists among people that results in differences in perceptions, behaviors, reactions to situations, and practices, it is essential to honor diversity to foster excellent communication, coexistence, practical learning, and behavior development.

One of the most significant challenges faced in the classroom is the ability to communicate to a multicultural audience. When teachers identify and anticipate gaps in cultural values, they will often be able to foster stronger conversations with parents. It is vital to identify them and create necessary mitigation steps before challenges that may affect learning.

Some of the differences in cultural perspectives that educators need to be on the lookout for include beliefs around relationships with the community, respect for authority figures, eye contact, and even personal space. Being intentional in identifying these differences can foster cultural sensitivity and awareness. This way, you will ensure significant aspects of learners' identities are not neglected during the learning process.

INTERACTIVE SELF-PRACTICE EXERCISES

1. Identify four common types of cultural diversity that exist in your classroom.

2. Describe two techniques to foster cultural sensitivity and awareness in the classroom that you can utilize immediately.

EFFECTIVE CONVERSATIONAL POINTS

1. With a colleague, discuss how cultural disparities show up in your school. Have a conversation that will motivate a deeper dive into exploring how cultural gaps manifest in the classroom. This can manifest in the ways students learn or behave. Explore how the gaps impact interactions between teachers and parents and how the interactions can be more effective.

2. Continue the conversation to investigate what you might do to unlearn practices that play down the diversity in multicultural learning, thinking, practices, and values. How would this affect your interactions with the parents? Would you do something differently?

   (a) Here, educators can explore opportunities also to recruit and create a space for culturally diverse educators to represent different groups in the classroom. Educators can also take the initiative to know their students better and, therefore, speak more knowledgeably with their parents.

   (b) Educators also can create diversity in their lesson plans and do away with teaching practices that do not acknowledge the reality of cultural diversity. This also can provide opportunities to tap into the strengths and talents of multicultural students and develop them and have tangible culturally relevant student work that can be highlighted when talking with parents.

NOTES

1. Van Eeden-Moorefield, B. and Demo, D.H. (2007). Family diversity. In: *Blackwell Encyclopedia of Sociology* (ed. G. Ritzer). Hoboken, NJ: Wiley-Blackwell.

2. Hoefstede, G. (2003). *Culture's Consequences: Comparing Values, Behaviors, Institutions and Organizations Across Nations, Second Edition*. Thousand Oaks, CA: Sage Publications.

8

WORKING WITH MULTICULTURAL FAMILIES

As the multicultural makeup of the U.S. student population increases, meaningful and effective communication between teachers and families of diverse cultural backgrounds becomes more challenging. Norms and values tend to vary greatly across cultures. So, when considering relationships between teachers and students and parents from different cultures, an awareness of the diverse perspectives, experiences, beliefs, and styles of communication common to other cultures is imperative. Teachers who understand and are more sensitive to these differences will be more successful when communicating with multicultural families.

Furthermore, effective communication between educators and a student and their family is crucial for student success. This is true across the board. However, in the case of multicultural students, it then becomes necessary to examine what effective communication looks like between teachers and parents of different ethnic backgrounds. That way, potential conflicts and misunderstandings can be avoided or at least decreased in degree or in the number of instances.

Often, teachers must take the different cultural values of ethnically diverse students and their families into account when communicating. Of equal importance is the teacher's ability to convey the school's culture to the parents so they understand what is academically and socially expected of their child in the classroom. A mutual cultural understanding between teachers and parents creates an environment where students can more easily learn and thrive.

Specific training in teacher-parent communication, particularly across cultural gaps, is often unavailable.[1] As a result, teachers must take it upon themselves to learn these skills and develop ways to communicate and build trust with multicultural families. This positive relationship and trust can easily translate to better student academic achievement.

This chapter raises awareness about the challenges associated with communication between teachers and families from multiethnic backgrounds and how to overcome them. Utilizing the previously reviewed Inglehart–Welzel axes of cultural values and Geert Hofstede's research on values dimensions, we look at how cultural differences play out in education settings and provide strategies to build stronger relationships between teachers and parents.

KEY DIMENSIONS OF CROSS-CULTURAL VARIATION RELATED TO PARENTS

Effective communication across cultures begins with understanding. Variation in beliefs, values, and behavior from culture to culture can make communication difficult. Understanding the root of many cultural differences can help bridge gaps in communication between teachers and families from multiethnic backgrounds.

As noted earlier, the Inglehart–Welzel work on the World Values Survey looks at variations in cultures along two major axes: traditional versus secular-rational and survival versus self-expression.[2]

Traditional values include religion, family, nationalism, social conformity, and deference to authority. People from these cultures tend to be socially conservative and reject divorce, suicide, abortion, and euthanasia. The secular-rational dimension does not place rigid importance on religion, family, nationalism, social conformity, and deference to authority. Instead, these populations tend to be socially progressive and more accepting of social liberties.

In the survival group, values are shaped by a history of existential insecurity and strict limits on human autonomy. There is a strong cultural emphasis on physical and economic security. This gives rise to support for authoritarian government and intolerance of sexual and gender freedom. Survival values seem to come from living in a society where survival is not necessarily a given, thus cultural diversity feels threatening. For this reason, people often stick with what is familiar and perceived to be non-threatening: traditional gender and sexual roles and rejection of the *other* (e.g., LGBTQ, divorce).

The self-expression group has developed in postindustrial societies where existential security and autonomy levels are high. Subjective well-being, autonomy, self-expression, acceptance of diversity, tolerance, and quality of life are central tenets of the value system. People in these societies want to have a say in the laws that govern their lives. Generally, postindustrial societies include conditions where survival is not a concern, so people feel comfortable moving on from traditional beliefs and ways of life to accommodate new and diverse perspectives. In the past several decades, postindustrial societies have seen a massive cultural shift toward equality in terms of gender, sexual orientation, and ethnic *others* as a result.

Although there are several conservative postindustrial countries and, in the United States, certain traditional political leanings live in a postindustrial society, generally speaking, cultural attitudes are usually strong indicators of one or the other of these group values. For example, societies that place significant value on religion tend to also highly value family, nationalism, and respect for authority. In other words, traditional values often correlate with survival values. On the other hand, an emphasis on secular-rational values tends to correlate with an emphasis on self-expression values.

Collectivism and Individualism

Another significant dimension in cross-cultural variation is that of collectivism versus individualism. Collectivist values give priority to the group or the collective over the individual. Individualist values give priority to the individual over the collective. Understanding the common values of collectivist cultures versus individualist cultures can help inform effective communication between teachers and multicultural families.

For example, research suggests that collectivist versus individualist values can predict the priority of the other values. Collectivists tend to be more religious and conservative. They value tradition, conformity, security, and certainty and are less open to change. People in collectivist societies generally do not prioritize their own needs and desires. They subscribe to an interdependent view of the self, where cooperation, connection, and harmony are the priority.

For example, when a Japanese family felt wronged by an advisor at a school who they found out later had failed to write a recommendation letter on time for the student to get admitted to a highly sought after summer program, they preferred to keep the harmony and not bring it up to the teacher. They were also worried that confronting the teacher could lead to a backlash against them, or their family would look like one who likes to stir up trouble, which they would feel is a negative image on them.

However, the opposite is not necessarily true for individualists. For example, when a teacher forgot to submit a recommendation letter, a parent embodying more of the individualist values confronted the teacher and explained what happened. The teacher was profusely apologetic and tried to make it up to the family. The actions of the parents could have been because of their personalities more than the cultural values, but as culture does influence individual traits, these respective reactions are not uncommon,

Social organization varies across cultures, particularly in terms of family and authority. Many collectivist cultures view family as the most important aspect of life. The needs of the family are considered more important than the needs of the individual. Child-rearing practices shape the identity of an individual to see oneself through the lens of the family unit first.[3] This is true in many collectivist cultures, including Mexico, Korea, China, India, and the Dominican Republic. Loyalty to family is the priority, and thus the opinions and efforts of teachers can be devalued by these families.

This is not the case, generally speaking, in Middle Eastern cultures, as educators are seen as high-ranking authority figures over children. Because of this, Arab parents often expect teachers to be moral, spiritual, and academic role models both in and out of the classroom. This might seem to put a lot of pressure on teachers, but the flip side is that Arab parents enter the relationship with trust and the goal of supporting teachers.[4] They also tend to participate heavily in their child's education. It is important to keep in mind that different school types and the locations of the schools often cultivate a different perception between parents and teachers.

Another changing factor is the digital age, which is transforming culture globally, and individualistic and collectivistic tendencies are shifting as shown by inconsistent findings when measuring cultural values. Within regions of a country that is largely one or the other may also differ. For example, Native American tribes in the United States may hold collectivist values but support individuality and not individualism. Families adapting traditionally collectivistic or individualistic cultures may also not follow those values rigidly. Teachers should be aware of these nuances.

Furthermore, making broad generalizations about the culture of a family simply because they're from a certain country is not an ideal approach. Understanding cultural tendencies can help teachers communicate better with multicultural families, without overreaching and making assumptions about them. Instead, keeping in mind the cultural tendencies of a student's family can help teachers choose the correct words and cultivate the proper tone of conversations. This is especially true when first getting to know a student and their family.

MAKING USE OF WHAT YOU KNOW

Using this kind of information to modify how teachers communicate with students and parents from family-focused cultures can result in better trust and comfort. For example, Marina worked with a family of Korean immigrants where the eldest sister was perpetually late for her morning class, resulting in a warning notice from the school. When pressed, the eldest sister revealed that she was late because both her parents were working, and she had the responsibility of taking her younger sister to preschool. When this situation was explained fully to the school administration, they worked with her to create an alternative school schedule to have the first period free.

As implied through this example, avoiding an individualistic and accusatory approach is critical when approaching any family, and particularly one from a collectivist background. Taking the family at large into account helps cultivate a meaningful and trusting teacher-parent relationship while addressing the issue at the same time.

Furthermore, when talking with parents, it's helpful to understand cultural influences that affect academic performance. For example, in some cultures, students have been taught to care more about the answer to a problem rather than focusing on the process of how they got it. This type of results-oriented thinking can cause issues in the classroom, where American teachers want students to show their work. However, the students feel frustrated when they provide the correct answer but lose points for not showing their work. Recognizing the discrepancy between ideologies, teachers can explain to these students why showing the work is an important part of the learning process, and doing so gives the teachers opportunities to understand how the student thinks, and gives opportunities for teachers to show students how they can leverage that strength in group projects, as some examples. These responses can also be shared with parents so they can better support this kind of learning at home.

Additionally, some cultures, like Korea, have a hierarchical language system based on age, status, and gender. Sometimes, this could appear like bullying. In one of Marina's cultural fluency classes, she taught the students how to use this language in a way that is not and won't resemble bullying, especially having observed many students get expelled from school because of this misunderstanding. The students lacked mentorship on how not to use the higher status of age onto a younger student properly, so he ordered the younger student around on occasion as his personal servant. On another occasion, there was an actual misunderstanding where the boy called the other *hyung* (which means "older brother," a common term to address members even outside the family structure). The teacher, having heard about Korean boys bullying each other, grabbed the older boy and demanded his response to, "Are you bullying this kid?" Both were shocked. The younger one saw the older one as a mentor (*sunbae*) to him and defended him on his behalf. In another similar instance, a teacher commented about the student's bullying tendency to the parents, which shocked them as they strongly encouraged kindness and respect to others. Such misunderstandings can cause significant unnecessary stress to a family and to the student, and some may feel that they are victims of discrimination.

In parts of India, Latin America, Africa, and some Native American societies, tribal culture represents a fairly significant portion of the population. The Indigenous communities of these regions account for hundreds of millions of people. Tribal cultures have unique cultural patterns, so the school culture versus the family culture of the student is likely to contrast greatly. This can cause problems with academics, discipline, and social behavior, which the teacher will have to navigate. Further navigation with the student's family can also be complex, as differing values contribute to different behavior and expectations. Because the family home does not resemble the classroom, student success is usually contingent on teachers bridging that gap.

- **India.** Tribal communities, of which there are roughly 573, speak their own languages, follow their own unique traditions, and often rely solely on natural resources to live. Most people in these communities are illiterate and resist modern education.[5]

- **Latin America.** Between Latin America and the Caribbean, roughly 826 Indigenous communities exist, totaling about 58 million people. Of those, only between 1 and 7 million live isolated in rural forest areas, while the rest live in more urban communities. Those isolated in rural areas suffer extremely high levels of poverty, where only around 43% of the population above age 15 has finished primary school.[6]

- **Africa.** Around 50 million Indigenous people live on the continent of Africa, most of whom are nomadic or partially nomadic with a hunter-gatherer lifestyle. There is a significant education gap between Indigenous and non-Indigenous people in Africa. For instance, in Cameroon, only about 1.31% of Indigenous Baka children attend primary school.[7]

- **Native Americans.** In the United States, there are 574 federally recognized Indigenous Nations, 229 of which are in Alaska. The education gap between Native American students and their non-Native peers has increased over the past decade, with Native students graduating from high school at a rate of less than 50% in some states,[8] due to both lack of school quality and the difficult socioeconomic factors facing Native families.

As mentioned, tribal cultures often embrace vastly different values than mainstream cultures. For this reason, education for students from some Indigenous tribes and cultures remains challenging. To be successful, collaboration between educators and parents is necessary. In this situation, effective communication begins with systemic changes that take tribal cultures into account when developing teaching methods for this student population. Because tribal cultures have historically been told they are obsolete and lesser-than, a teacher who makes an effort to understand and consider their values and incorporate them into the student's education can go a long way.

Communicating with the parents of students from tribal cultures often requires forethought and sensitivity to be successful. Consider the situation where a Native American student from a tribal culture never participates in class. This might be because it is common in many Native American cultures to learn by observation rather than trial-and-error.

Rather than approach the parent with an accusatory tone, it will likely be more effective to begin the conversation as follows:

> *Your son has excellent observation skills. His way of learning appears to use observation as the primary component. It would be helpful in my class environment if he could complement his observational skills by adding on some additional learning practices regarding participation. Participating in class discussions will help him become more engaged with the material and may even cement some of the information more firmly in his mind. When students contribute their own ideas to what we're learning, that connection helps them remember the information! Also, his contributions will be beneficial for the whole class, as other students can start thinking about things from his perspective as he shares his ideas.*

Saying something along these lines accomplishes several things. First of all, it shows that learning through observation, a behavior he likely learned at home, is also valuable. The teacher does not frame their own style of learning as more valuable. Instead, they situate both together as complementary learning styles. The teacher's explanation also shows they are thinking about how the student will benefit and how the classroom will benefit from his participation. This may allow the parents to see the teacher as a caring resource for their child as well as all students, which can help cultivate a trusting teacher-parent relationship in the long term.

CULTURAL-DEFICIT VERSUS ASSET MODEL

Many teachers find it helpful to view interactions with others from various cultural backgrounds with the viewpoint of the Cultural-Asset versus a Cultural-Deficit model. The latter sees individuals in minority groups as lacking in certain values, skills, etc., compared to the majority group; the former sees the unique cultural values of minorities as an asset. The script above reflects the positive perspective.

Showing how this can be done is also important. As stated in an earlier chapter, showing examples of how you can encourage students in the classroom (warm-up activities, oral assignments, etc.) gives confidence to the parent that you are giving tools to students to learn how to participate more. Often the students want to participate.

Again, it is necessary to reiterate that widening your cultural understanding as an educator does not translate to using generalizations as the primary basis for communication with multiethnic families. The goal of understanding different cultures is to use it to inform your language and communication style where appropriate.

CONSIDERING CULTURAL GAPS

In practice, using cultural background information to inform your communication style with multiethnic families can manifest in many ways. Knowing how to best apply this knowledge depends on the context of the situation.

For example, consider Western individualist cultures and the perception of control. Many people from individualist cultures tend to feel they have a lot of control over their environment, which influences how they feel about goal achievement, physical health, and mental health. This leads to more assertiveness in individual behavior. When you believe you have control over a situation, you place a lot of weight on your actions. Thus, being assertive is a way of maneuvering the experience to fit your goals.

In contrast, collectivist cultures do not have this same cultural ideology. Some students and parents from primarily collectivist cultures tend to believe they don't have control over many situations, as they have been primed to accept an external locus of control. Keeping this difference in mind can help to better navigate conversations with families from more collectivist cultures.

Take, for example, a conversation between a teacher and a parent from Japan (a traditionally collectivist culture) where the student is not performing well academically due to continued distractions from fellow students. If the teacher simply indicates the student is getting a C in the class as a way of saying the student is not performing well academically, that might not frame the situation in a way the parent will be able to understand. They might think the teacher isn't giving adequate instruction, and that is why their child isn't performing well academically, viewing the situation from a more collectivist lens. Instead, a higher probability of success will come from initiating the conversation as follows:

> *We're currently starting a new unit looking at animal biology, and all the students have individual assignments to dissect frogs. Your daughter has a wonderful rapport with her fellow students and is always very helpful to those who are struggling to understand the material. I have noticed that she can spend a lot of her energies in conversations with others during class time, and it is important to bring this up to you.*
>
> *Your daughter is clearly a student with strong potential and excellent analytical ability. She has the ability to do well in this class, and I would like your assistance in helping her to find ways to focus better during classroom sessions. I know her friendships are very important to her, and I'm glad that she is doing so*

well socially. However, her grades are starting to slip to a level that is beneath her potential. I am planning on moving the classroom seating to remove some of the distractions for her and wanted to let you know this in advance. Do you have any ideas for how we might work together to support your daughter to do better?

Using this approach can develop a strong relationship with the parent and move the process of student support forward in a positive direction. By initially discussing the broader context of what is occurring in the classroom (rather than focusing directly on the individual), the teacher frames the conversation through collectivist perspectives, putting the parent on more comfortable terrain. Providing actions to be taken by the student, teacher, and parent all helps the parent to see that everyone is working as a team for the solution.

Uncertainty avoidance, or tolerance for things being unpredictable, is another factor to consider when communicating with multiethnic parents. When mapping this dimension onto the survival versus self-expression axis, survivalist cultures tend to be more attuned to avoiding uncertainty. Therefore, providing a predictable learning path may be helpful when communicating with families from these cultures. The more predictability you can provide, the more confidence many parents will have in the educator.

Another common cultural gap is the perception of time. For example, in Mexico, cultural norms regarding time are much different than the ones in the United States. Mexico has a more time-relaxed culture, where people often don't operate on an exact schedule. Time is more fluid. If someone says they will arrive at 10:00 a.m., they might arrive at 10:15 a.m. and not consider themselves late. However, in the United States, a person who arrives 15 minutes after the scheduled time would be considered late in almost all circumstances. Understanding this can be helpful to avoid frustration when meeting with a Mexican family or disciplining a Mexican student.

Gender egalitarianism is a relatively new cultural construct even in the West. Many cultures around the globe don't subscribe to the concept of gender equality, and it's important to consider this when communicating with multiethnic families. This can manifest in many different ways. For example, some cultures have traditionally put more pressure on their sons' achievement over their daughters. While norms are shifting somewhat, the heightened emphasis on male education remains largely true for many Chinese and Arab families. In these situations, using softer language or tone when discussing issues with a son's academics or behavior both can take some of the weight off of the student as well as help ensure the parents don't feel insulted by the comments.

Many individuals in a "being" or collectivist culture define themselves by their relationship to their community, considering their family line as the principal factor in who they are over the individual self. One Korean student with whom Marina worked closely was expelled from his boarding school for repeated drinking offenses. His main regret was not the impact on his life, but the dishonor he had caused to his family.

Of course, there is fluidity in family identity. In "doing" or individualist cultures, the individual defines themselves by their own accomplishments and earned status. Considering the extent to which a family with a different ethnic background is part of a "being" versus "doing" culture can be helpful in communication. For instance, talking with parents about a student, contextualizing the student as part of their family rather than speaking about them in isolation can make some parents feel more comfortable, trusting, and understood by a teacher. What's more, framing the classroom environment as a "family" can help some students feel more included.

Collectivist cultures have different norms with regard to independence and privacy than individualist cultures. Privacy within the family is not a priority in collectivist cultures. In the context of education, understanding that certain students will have no privacy from their parents can influence the type or subject matter of homework given. Furthermore, a teacher who understands this element of certain cultures is less likely to be caught off guard if parents want especially detailed accounts of class activities and assignments as well as their child's performance and behavior.

Students can develop different learning styles based on what is modeled at home. The majority of Native American communities situate respect for elders as a central component of their culture. For this reason, an observational rather than hands-on style of learning can be more common in Native American students.

Along the same lines, a student who constantly talks out of turn may not realize this is considered misbehavior because of the cultural dynamic at home, where talking over one another is normal. Before addressing an issue with the parents, understanding if a behavior comes from a cultural norm picked up from their family will help to address the situation most effectively. What's more, it may serve as a cue to teachers for how their own cultural values might be influencing the way they teach.

Some cultures highly value formality and privacy, which teachers should consider when communicating with multiethnic families. For example, in Slavic culture, the norm is to be formal, reserved, and private. As such, in communication with Slavic parents, remaining formal, only discussing relevant information about the student, and avoiding personal topics is a general guideline to keep in mind.

Using purposeful language in conversations with parents is another decision teachers can make to create a positive relationship with multiethnic families. For example, parents from family-focused, collectivist cultures might appreciate a teacher addressing an achievement or issue with their child in the context of the family. Saying something like, "The family should be proud," or "This is something the family will need to consider moving forward," can be more effective at getting a message across than addressing the achievement or issue as the child's individual success or failure. On the flip side, being aware of the level of shame avoidance for families can be helpful when handling negative instances. For many Japanese families, hearing about a student's misbehaviors would be seen as a reason for familial shame to an extent that hinders fruitful communication. To mitigate the potential negative impact in these situations, educators can use more collectivist language about students in general misbehaving or allude to the difficulties faced by a teacher when students are not fully attentive. For example, a teacher could say, "Some students have had challenges in —, and what I'd advise those families that they appreciated and worked well for the student was —." This can also be used for students who may have learning difficulties.

COMMON DISCREPANCIES IN CULTURAL PERSPECTIVES

People's behavior is influenced by their culture. What might be considered polite in one culture easily could be construed as rude in another. Making note of some of these differences can help teachers navigate conversations with multicultural families. Below are some common discrepancies in cultural perspectives.

Eye contact. In some cultures, eye contact indicates engagement and attention, and a lack of eye contact can be interpreted as disrespect. However, in many East Asian cultures, avoiding eye contact can be a way to demonstrate your acceptance of the implied hierarchy.

Directness in communication. Some cultures find directness to indicate respect, and in other cultures it is the opposite, where being direct can be considered rude or a violation of boundaries. These differences can be apparent immediately when conversing with traditional Indian families, who mince few words in their assessment of their children, as opposed to traditional Chinese families, who may tend to be extremely circumspect.

Role of teachers. Some cultures regard teachers as an automatic authority, whereas in others, teachers are supposed to earn the family's respect. This can be seen in the level of respect immediately afforded to teachers by many East Asian families, as opposed to families from a White American background, who may see teaching as a less attractive profession.

Physical space and boundaries. Standing close to someone can either be a sign of trust or a violation of personal space, depending on the culture. For Latin American families, close personal contact is a loose norm, and casual touches on greetings are usually acceptable, if not necessarily expected. For families from Middle Eastern backgrounds, meanwhile, maintaining physical distance between opposite genders is of paramount importance. While many families will be forgiving of unintentional blunders, a little forethought can go a long way.

SUMMARY

Teachers who put in the effort to understand different cultures can directly translate to more seamless and effective communication with multiethnic families. A person's cultural background often influences their ideology and behavior, so a teacher who can see these potential differences is better able to engage in effective and meaningful conversation with parents.

That being said, having cultural information about an ethnic group or nationality does not provide a one-size-fits-all template for teacher-parent communication. Every family is unique, and it is impossible to know if or how much their cultural background applies to their actual ideology and behavior. Understanding various cultural norms can bridge some cultural gaps, but teachers should never use stereotypes and generalizations to make blanket assumptions about a family.

INTERACTIVE SELF-PRACTICE EXERCISES

1. Select three elements in the following list and research what are some common characteristics of the cultural dimensions, and which countries and ethnicities have traditionally adopted these values.

    (a) Include an example of individualism and collectivism.
    (b) Survival and self-expression.
    (c) Traditional and secular-rational values.
    (d) Masculinity-femininity.
    (e) Power distance.
    (f) Uncertainty avoidance.
    (g) Indulgence-restraint.

2. Select one norm you were brought up with. Dig into what events (both familial and cultural) originated to make up this norm.

    (a) Now, consider your opinions, values, customs, and behaviors and link them to norms in your culture.
    (b) Note both the similarities and differences.
    (c) What are some of your attributes/ideas that are aligned with your culture?
    (d) What are some that are not?

EFFECTIVE CONVERSATIONAL POINTS

1. Consider the different traditional cultural norms of collectivist and individualist cultures.

   (a) What factors do you think influence how accurate those norms will be reflected in a family? Consider things like wealth, whether they're from an urban or rural area, etc.

2. What role do you think technology, social media, and digital globalization play in influencing cultural values and norms? How do you see traditional cultural norms shifting in the coming generations because of the internet? In what ways is the internet causing global culture to bypass regional culture in younger generations? Is this positive or negative? Analyzing these ideas might make accidental stereotyping less common. (You also might ask the same question using different cross-cultural dimensions as well.)

3. Interacting with students and their families from another culture, what are some of the initial things you can do to get to know them?

   (a) For example, do you think having both the student and a parent fill out a questionnaire about their cultural and religious background, expectations, availability (for parents), and home language would help foster a positive relationship between teacher and parent?

   (b) Why would something like this be helpful? Why might it not be a good idea?

NOTES

1. Trumbull, E., Rothstein-Fisch, C., and Hernandez, E. (2003). Parent involvement in schooling—according to whose values? *School Community Journal* 13: 45–73. https://www.researchgate.net/publication/268254869_Parent_Involvement_in_Schooling-According_to_Whose_Values.

2. Inglehart, R. and Welzel, C. (2005). *Modernization, Cultural Change and Democracy: The Human Development Sequence.* New York: Cambridge University Press (Chapter 2). https://www.researchgate.net/publication/230557603_Modernization_Cultural_Change_and_Democracy_The_Human_Development_Sequence.

3. Yi, J.S. (2018). Revisiting individualism-collectivism: a cross-cultural comparison among college students in four countries. *Journal of Intercultural Communication.*

4. Cukur, C.S., Guzman, M.R., and Carlo, G. (2004). Religiosity, values, and horizontal and vertical individualism-collectivism: a study of Turkey, the United States, and the Philippines. *Journal of Social Psychology* 144 (6): 613–364.

5. Kapur, R. (2018). Challenges of education amongst the tribals in India. https://researchgate.net/publication/323691659_Challenges_of_Education_amongst_the_Tribals_in_India.

6. Food and Agriculture Organization of the United Nations. (n.d.). Who are the indigenous and tribal peoples of Latin America and the Caribbean? https://www.fao.org/3/cb2953en/online/src/html/who-are-the-indigenous-and-tribal-peoples-of-latin-america-and-the-caribbean.html.

7. UN Department of Public Information. (2013). Indigenous people in the African region. https://www.un.org/esa/socdev/unpfii/documents/2013/Media/Fact%20Sheet_Africa_%20UNPFII-12.pdf.

8. Morgan, H. (2009). What every teachers needs to know to teach Native American students. *Multicultural Education* 16 (4): 10–12. https://files.eric.ed.gov/fulltext/EJ858583.pdf.

PART III

REMEMBERING THE INDIVIDUAL

9

MAKING SPACE
FOR INDIVIDUAL
SELF-ACTUALIZATION

The actions of each individual student and family member, of course, are not completely determined by their inclusion in a particular cultural group. Core beliefs and values influence how different cultures perceive the world, build relationships, and interact both inside and outside of their defined groups.

However, these core beliefs are not practiced and internalized equally among individuals in the group. Educators are well served to seek a balance between being mindful of cultural backgrounds while creating space for the individual to demonstrate their own unique personality and ways of expression, thereby assisting each student under their care to make steps toward their own growth.

The longstanding model of needs first posited by Abraham Maslow in 1943[1] provides a useful framework for educators to assist individual students to move forward within their own cultural context. Maslow put forth a system that classified the universal needs of society. As shown in Figure 9.1, this system is often framed as a pyramid, with primary needs at the base.

The concept of self-actualization tops Maslow's hierarchy of needs pyramid and requires the most work to achieve. According to Maslow, one can only achieve self-actualization once

Figure 9.1   Maslow's pyramid of needs.

Source: Adapted from *Journal of Transpersonal Psychology*, 1969.

the more basic needs are first met. Self-actualized individuals are the ones who accept who they are, regardless of the limitations and experience, and, through this, unlock their full potential.

Individuals who achieve self-actualization share similar characteristics like the ability to build deep relationships, appreciate life, and engage in truly meaningful work. Helping students to achieve self-actualization is perhaps the most important role of an educator, as this unlocks the full development of an individual.

IMPORTANCE OF SELF-ACTUALIZATION

Self-actualization is the innate development of an individual to achieve their full potential, control their destiny, and feel a sense of purpose in their lives. Self-actualization is achieved when basic and other needs in the hierarchy of needs theory, such as safety and esteem needs, are met. Individuals tend to prepare better and tolerate uncertainties if they are self-actualized. Through self-actualization, people also can perceive reality more efficiently, making it possible to accept others and themselves how they are.

Students who have achieved self-actualization are spontaneous both in action and thought, making them more flexible, creative, and fulfilled. When people achieve self-actualization, their progression beyond the basic needs allows them to become problem-centered as opposed to self-centered. Their outlook on life becomes objective, making them rational thinkers and work abstractly by considering concepts beyond what is physically observable. As they have progressed beyond the level of primary needs, self-actualized individuals are usually concerned about humanity and are more likely to appreciate life.

Self-actualized students are more capable of taking a creative approach to problem-solving, as they do not get "stuck" on solutions that only resolve basic needs or focus on individual gain. They appreciate and acknowledge the benefits that come with helping others solve problems. They are also empathetic and have more clarity on what is right and wrong. Another valuable characteristic that makes self-actualized students better problem solvers is their openness to contrasting views.

By supporting the self-actualization of their students, educators are able to create classrooms that foster and support collaboration, particularly in cross-cultural settings. Students who reach a higher degree of self-actualization are open to new and fresh perspectives. No matter how similar an experience of others may be to them, they are willing to look through others' lenses and appreciate the diversity of ideas and experiences. This gives them a great capacity to be collaborative and creative.

Self-actualization plays a critical role in helping individuals have optimal experiences, which are helpful to their existence. This comprises positive relations with others, autonomy, personal growth, identifying their purpose, and self-acceptance, fostering positive learning dynamics within the classroom. Additionally, the healthy perspective on life brought about by achieving self-actualization helps students to form deeper interpersonal relationships and live up to higher ethical standards.

VARIATIONS OF SELF-ACTUALIZATION ACROSS INDIVIDUALISTIC AND COLLECTIVIST CULTURES

According to Maslow's theory, the greatest need is the need to achieve one's full potential. The way in which this need is fulfilled is highly personal, varying across individuals and cultures. For instance, while one student would make steps toward self-actualization by working to support their family, another may see themselves as reaching their potential through running a marathon, and another by going to college.

Educators working to support students to achieve self-actualization should consider the cultural background from which the student is coming and tailor the approach accordingly. Maslow's hierarchy of needs theory can be applied in both individualistic and collective cultures, though the ways in which self-actualization is achieved can vary.[2] For instance, in a collectivist culture, the basic need is belongingness. Self-esteem is eliminated as a need, while self-actualization may be achieved when societal or group needs are achieved. This can be illustrated in the case of one Korean student with whom Marina worked extensively, who put off her studies in computer science in order to care for her ailing father. While this form of self-sacrifice was difficult for her Western peers to understand, her behavior was in line with self-actualization within a more collectivist culture. Therefore, contrary to the belief that self-actualization needs apply the same way to individuals, they are bound by culture to an extent.

Students coming from individualized cultures are often expected to achieve self-actualization independent of their group's social structures. The high value within these cultures on self-sufficiency, self-definition, and independence cultivates social behaviors motivated by individual desires, prioritizing personal achievement above group success. Indeed, a common cliché within individualized societies is for the successful person to "rise above" their particular background.

The motivation and cognition of individuals in a collectivist culture, meanwhile, are driven by the social systems they exist in. Collectivistic individuals are focused on others, and their motivation is driven by approval by their groups, adherence to social systems, and acceptance by others. While the focus of individualistic persons may be on achieving personal happiness, collectivistic individuals are focused on achieving something good for society. They rarely think of themselves as individuals. This, thus, creates a difference in how self-actualization needs are viewed or applied in collectivistic groups.

APPLICATIONS IN EDUCATION

Maslow's hierarchy of needs theory is designed to address the obscure and basic needs of human existence. One cannot achieve a higher-order need when the lower-order needs are not fulfilled. Thus, an individual needs to meet physiological needs such as food before moving to safety and self-esteem needs, for instance.

Self-actualization needs are at the peak of the hierarchy of the needs pyramid and have proven to be the hardest to achieve. The Maslow hierarchy of needs motivational theory serves as a developmental model that can be utilized across cross-cultural settings, as long as educators are mindful of how actualization may differ according to core beliefs.

Self-actualization can be applied in education to support academic success and enhance the quality of educational experiences for both educators and learners. Teachers can use the model to enhance the quality of learning for students in a way that helps unlock higher-order thinking for enhanced performance. Regardless of cultural background, students who have achieved self-actualization feel able to autonomously explore and make discoveries independently. They can derive meaning from learning and apply it in real life by getting the most out of the classroom experience. They tend be more creative, and participate in self-expressive projects.

Supporting learners to reach self-actualization starts by being mindful of the progression from basic to advanced needs, as the foundation must be put in place for higher-level needs to be achieved. Some of the initiatives educators can put in place to help learners achieve their physiological needs include being mindful of the timing for student's meals and drinks, allowing bathroom breaks, and providing clean classrooms and facilities that ensure the students are comfortable. Security and safety needs can be ensured by maintaining control of classroom behavior, adopting nonthreatening attitudes, and demonstrating consistent rules for discipline.

To assist students to meet the higher-level needs of belongingness and esteem, it may be necessary to understand the cultural background of the particular student. Learners coming from collectivist cultural backgrounds, including many East Asian and Latin American families, may have strong support structures already in place to achieve belonging within their extended family and community, as the cultural value on belonging can manifest in stronger group bonds.

While avoiding making any assumptions, educators can ask general questions about the role of family and other groups in the student's life, to determine if their needs for belonging are being met. Regardless of cultural background, educators can sustain a sense of belonging for students by allowing them to be heard and showing them that their opinions and thoughts are valued. Making efforts to know each student provides models and space to encourage the students to be interested in knowing each other, thereby creating the classroom as a space for belongingness and connection.

Self-esteem can be a more keenly felt need for students from more individualistic cultures, which may include those from Northern European or White American backgrounds. Educators can empower these learners to achieve self-esteem by developing award programs, encouraging them to focus on their strengths, recognizing a job well done, and giving out individual responsibilities.

For students from more collectivist cultures, meanwhile, educators may be well served to remain mindful of the value placed on modesty and humility within these backgrounds.

Efforts to acknowledge individual students for praise or rewards may not result in heightened self-esteem, but rather shame in being singled out. Instead, educators may help those students meet their needs for self-esteem by highlighting the positive attributes and achievements of the class as a whole, and making reference to the collaboration and inclusion that resulted in positive outcomes for all.

Ultimately, by demonstrating empathy, compassion, being accommodative, being positive, and creating a supportive environment, teachers can help all students realize their full potential.

SUMMARY

Maslow's hierarchy of needs theory of motivation can be applied in the classroom environments to encourage development. Achieving self-actualization has benefits both for the individual student and peers. Self-actualized students tend to demonstrate acceptance, empathy, and support more, creating an environment that encourages creativity, harmony, and growth.

Self-actualization can be applied in educational settings. Educators can use Maslow's hierarchy of needs to examine how their actions can help their students meet their needs and realize their full potential. However, as educators apply the theory, they must learn how to vary their approach and understand what reaching full potential may mean. Self-actualization can manifest differently in individualist and collectivistic cultures.

INTERACTIVE SELF-PRACTICE EXERCISES

1. Identify the cultures represented in your school. For each, use your background research to determine if the culture can be considered primarily individualistic or collectivistic. Conduct short interviews with students to identify how individuals perceive self-actualization.

2. Using this research, create a model to help you apply Maslow's theory.
   (a) List the five needs, from the lower-order needs to self-actualization.
   (b) Classify the needs into deficiency and growth needs.
   (c) Evaluate every need and identify which ones have been met and to what extent.
   (d) Create a model you can use to empower students to achieve their needs.

EFFECTIVE CONVERSATIONAL POINTS

1. With a colleague, discuss what students need to do their best in your school. Identify the current needs and classify them in the order of Maslow's model.

2. With a colleague, discuss the methods you have seen be successful to empower students to meet their deficiency and growth needs.

NOTES

1. Maslow, A. H. (1993) [1971]. Theory Z. In: *The Farther Reaches of Human Nature*. New York: Arkana, pp. 270–286. Reprinted from *Journal of Transpersonal Psychology* (1969) 1 (2): 31–47.
2. Ivtzan, I. (2008). Self actualisation: for individualistic cultures only? *International Journal on Humanistic Ideology* 1: 111–138.

10

ADDRESSING NEURODIVERSITY WITH CROSS-CULTURAL FAMILIES

Each student is a unique individual, with varied cognitive and processing functions that influence the ability to take in new information, behave in an acceptable fashion in social settings, develop meaningful relationships, and communicate effectively through verbal and nonverbal means.

The growing acceptance and understanding of individual differences in American society have built a conventional foundation for addressing these obstacles, giving educators and families some grounding for discussions and mutual support. However, families from different cultural backgrounds may either lack awareness or have misconceptions around their understanding of neurodiversity, creating true challenges for effective communication and student well-being.

This chapter provides an overview of common neurodevelopmental disorders and how families who hold different cultural values might perceive them differently. We review some ways educators commonly differentiate instruction to accommodate for neurodiversity and provide advice for how to effectively communicate these methods to cross-cultural families.

Given the sensitivity of the topic of cognitive functioning and processing ability, these can be highly charged conversations, and must be approached with care and compassion.

WHAT IS NEURODIVERSITY?

Despite the linkages with cognitive disabilities, everyone in fact has some measure of neurodiversity. For example, there is no specific measure of classroom concentration, implying that a teacher cannot use a single student as a point of reference when it comes to knowledge retention in a classroom setup. Some students may be able to process the information faster than others, but that does not mean they will have similar abilities to retain the same information.

That said, there are true challenges when working with students with neurodevelopmental disorders. This book is not a comprehensive guide for addressing students with neurodevelopmental disorders and should not be utilized in place of guidance with trained counselors and psychologists. For general reference, we provide a brief synopsis of neurodevelopmental disorders commonly diagnosed within students. Recent increases in diagnoses have been attributed to the improved ability of medical and psychological practitioners to recognize and address issues.

AUTISM SPECTRUM DISORDER (ASD) AND ASPERGER SYNDROME

While ASD is not regarded as a learning disability, it affects learning for the affected persons. Students with ASD usually have difficulties with joint attention, using eye contact and bodily gestures to share their experiences with others. The complications can make it challenging for the students to develop communication and language skills. The students may struggle with sensory processing and may avoid sensory input. The students may excel in logical thinking ability, memorizing and learning information, or learning to read at a very early age.

Asperger syndrome is often linked with autism, as a neurodevelopmental condition with somewhat similar (though lessened in intensity) characteristics, including difficulties in social interaction and nonverbal communication and restricted and repetitive patterns of behavior and interests.

ATTENTION DEFICIT HYPERACTIVITY DISORDER (ADHD)

Attention deficit hyperactivity disorder is a medical condition that impacts brain development and activity, affecting attention, sitting ability, and self-control. The common signs of

ADHD include inattentiveness and ease of distraction. Students with hyperactivity become restless, easily bored, and impulsive by acting too quickly before thinking. Students with ADHD usually have difficulty focusing, paying attention, or working hard on their schoolwork. Unless properly supported, students with ADHD symptoms have problems coping with repeated cycles of negative thoughts and worries, irregular lifestyles, self-dissatisfaction, and low self-esteem. Negative attitudes toward neurodiverse students lead to stigmatization, significantly impacting their academic performance.

DYSLEXIA

Dyslexia is a learning disorder that involves difficulty in reading due to challenges in identifying speech sounds and learning how to associate with others. The condition affects parts of the brain that process language. Students with dyslexia usually have difficulties recognizing and manipulating the sounds in language. The students have difficulty decoding new words, making them have reading, writing, and spelling challenges.

DYSCALCULIA

Dyscalculia is a learning disability in mathematics. Students with the disorder usually have difficulties performing calculations, weak mental arithmetic skills, and a poor sense of numbers and estimation. Students with dyscalculia usually find it difficult to learn math in the classroom as they have trouble doing basic mathematical calculations and memorizing timetables.

SPECIFIC STRATEGIES FOR TEACHING NEURODIVERSE STUDENTS

Neurodiverse students often have specific sensory, cognition, and social and emotional needs that require differentiated instruction from teachers. The following are instructional strategies related to each category.

Diverse learners with sensory needs may require physical activity or be sensitive to specific noises and textures.

- Allow students to wear headphones or earplugs in the classroom as needed to create a comfortable working environment for them.
- Be conscious of your speaking volume as a teacher.
- Be conscious of background noise and, if possible, figure out ways to control it.

- Give students timed breaks to physically move around a couple times throughout the class. Instruct them with movements that involve the whole body, like jumping jacks.

- When dealing with activities or tasks that require students to interact with objects that have a certain texture, provide alternate options so students with texture sensitivities are able to participate and learn as well.

- Keep fidget toys and weighted materials on hand in the classroom that students can use as needed.

- Replace fluorescent lights with lamps in the classroom (if allowed by school administration).

Diverse learners with cognition needs may require teachers to consider their memory, organization, and ability to process information when designing curriculum.

- Clearly state the learning objective before and after each lesson.

- Organize information through color coding.

- Utilize fonts that are easy to read in presentations and handouts.

- Create activities that are short and interactive.

- Relay information in smaller chunks.

- Stay flexible about timed tasks, as some students might take longer to process information and feel paralyzed by the stress of timed activities.

SOCIAL AND EMOTIONAL NEEDS

Teachers should consider the social and emotional needs of certain diverse learners when creating curriculum and adjusting the classroom environment.

- Allow students to choose who they work with during group work.

- Allow students to choose their own seats.

- Provide activities for practicing social skills.

- Affirm and reaffirm often that the classroom is a safe space to ask for help.

- Assign students with social and emotional needs a buddy in the class to provide individual support when needed.

- Clearly communicate specific expectations for each activity or lesson.

- Be conscious of the signs a student is becoming agitated or overwhelmed and figure out "calming corners" or other compassionate methods of response ahead of time.

ADDRESSING NEURODIVERSITY WITH CULTURAL SENSITIVITY

The Individuals with Disorders Education Act (IDEA) of the United States enables children, teenagers, and young adults aged 3 to 21 years to receive free public education if diagnosed with a recognized learning disability. The education act also mandates that schools provide learning environments, activities, and evaluations tailored to individual student needs. It is thus not unusual for instructors to have a class with various learning preferences and skills, such as children with varying cognitive capacities, hyperactivity, and emotional challenges. Maintaining a balance between impartiality, offering a fair and outstanding education to all, and adjusting to individual learning needs has become increasingly challenging for instructors.

This challenge can take on untold complexities when involving families from cultures with differing core beliefs or preconceptions around neurodiversity. One illustrative example comes from Marina's work with "Jonathan," an exceptionally talented and sensitive Korean teenager. Jonathan was raised in a stereotypically traditional Korean household, with a businessman father who expected his son to follow a similarly high-paying and prominent career field.

Both of Jonathan's parents were intensely focused on his academic success and believed the school and teachers should be foundational partners in pressuring him to succeed. When Jonathan's school counselor told his parents that he believed Jonathan exhibited signs of ADHD, they were shocked. Given their core beliefs in the lofty role of teachers, this diagnosis seemed to Jonathan's parents to be a poor excuse for being unable to adequately manage student behavior. For them, the concept of hyperactivity and information processing differences were translated into a lack of effort on Jonathan's part.

Jonathan's parents left the meeting disappointed in both the school and their son. Altering their conception required taking another tact entirely, first highlighting his creative abilities and empathic nature. Jonathan's attention disorder was then framed as a result of overtiredness due to high efforts expended on classwork, with counseling and medication posited as a highly socially acceptable and "American" intervention.

The immediate stigmatization seen in the example of Jonathan's parents worsens the gap between what is needed and the available resources to ensure the neurodiverse student's success. Therefore, the first step for classroom educators is to ensure efforts are made to develop awareness among parents and create a sense of inclusivity and understanding.

This can require a gradual approach, as one educator interviewed for this book from a Swiss school noted that the United States was easily 50 years "ahead" of the rest of the world in terms of comfort around discussing neurodiversity. She mentioned a key learning point for her around caution with making assumptions about what a parent might want for their neurodiverse child. This learning moment came when she asked the Filipino mother of an autistic child what her hopes and dreams were for her child's future. The educator made an error in expressing her assumption that the parents wished for her child to become independent. Given the tight familial bonds within Filipino culture, making reference to the child ever living alone was taken as a sign of disrespect and completely outside of the frame of reference for the family. From this incident, the educator learned to keep her approach toward open-ended questions only, using the parent's responses to frame all subsequent queries.

There are times when English language learners have been mistaken for students who require special ed, drastically changing the child's trajectory, both in terms of the child's relationship with the family and even its society as well as within their own academic paths. A school not having had many students learning English as a second language mistakenly interpreted the student's blank stares to questions and slow thinking (what they perceived but the child was translating long texts in his head) as needing special ed. Many parents of such students cannot advocate for themselves, either because of the language barrier or because they lack social capital. Unfortunately, some of those students are then placed in programs not appropriate to them, leaving parents feeling helpless.

USING A STRENGTHS-BASED MODEL

The strengths-based model is a holistic method of teaching that focuses on an individual's strengths rather than their deficits. With regard to neurodiverse students, this means taking their natural capabilities into consideration when designing a curriculum, pedagogy, lessons, and even the classroom environment. The result is a learning environment that allows the student to thrive both academically and socially, two important goals of any education setting. Highlighting the first can be particularly important when working with students from East Asian backgrounds, while noting the social benefits can be more attractive for families holding Latin American cultural values.

The strength-based teaching model for neurodiverse students cannot be applied without first knowing how to correctly identify their strengths. In this context, strengths can be divided into two categories: strengths the teacher or parents recognize and strengths the students see in themselves. This distinction is valuable in that teachers can work within the framework of the strengths the student exhibits to design a curriculum that also incorporates other strengths they might not realize they have.

For example, if a student realizes they have excellent reading comprehension, they will likely gravitate toward reading-based activities on their own. However, the teacher might also note they excel at solving math problems. The teacher could use their natural tendency to enjoy reading and leverage it, introducing reading-based math exercises to further develop their math skills. This way of creating curriculum takes the student's strong points into consideration.

The following categories represent numerous areas in which students can show strengths.[1] Each category also includes examples to demonstrate the kinds of things that can be included. Keep in mind that this list is not exhaustive, but a starting point to simplify identifying student strengths.

Personal Strengths

- Finds finishing tasks empowering.
- Good sense of humor.
- Excels working independently.
- Easily learns from mistakes.
- Strong sense of integrity.

Social Strengths

- Loves talking in front of groups of people.
- Finds it easy to trust others.
- Loyal friend.
- Good manners.
- Natural leader.

Emotional Strengths

- Strong sense of empathy.
- Does not let emotions cloud judgment.
- Optimistic attitude.
- Trusts their instincts.
- Good at cheering up others.

Communication Strengths

- Great at explaining complex ideas to others.
- Asks questions when they don't understand something.
- Accepts constructive criticism without taking it personally.

- Persuasive.
- Great storyteller.

Logical Strengths

- Excels at solving math problems.
- Makes accurate estimates quickly.
- Easily calculates numbers in their head.
- Loves playing mind puzzles.

Physical Strengths

- Great dancer.
- Excellent balance.
- Physically strong.
- Great at team sports.
- Very physically flexible.

Literacy Strengths

- Excellent reading comprehension.
- Large vocabulary.
- Excels at writing across genres.
- Fast reader.
- Easily picks up on themes and symbolism in literature.

Creative Strengths

- Plays a musical instrument well.
- Excels at drawing.
- Easily comes up with new ideas.
- Naturally imaginative.

Cognitive Strengths

- Very organized.
- Pays close attention to detail.
- Great at thinking ahead.

- Great at multitasking.
- Excellent memory.

Technology Strengths
- Conducts effective internet searches.
- Easily navigates new technologies.
- Knows how to code.
- Excels at video games.
- Excels at graphic design.

Spiritual Strengths
- Sees the beauty in everyday things.
- Loves thinking about life's big questions.
- Feels a strong sense of religious faith.
- Practices meditation and/or yoga.
- Strong sense of morality.

Visual-Spatial Strengths
- Excellent at reading maps.
- Easily able to fix things.
- Good sense of direction.
- Completes jigsaw puzzles with ease.

Miscellaneous Strengths
- Great cook.
- Good at managing money.
- Excellent sense of fashion.
- Natural entrepreneur.
- Great with animals.

Communicating these strengths to parents can be a powerful method to set a strong foundation as part of the conversation around alterations to curriculum and teaching methods. Certain of these strengths may have more saliency with particular cultural values, including the linkage of spiritualism with Native American and Middle Eastern cultures, and social and communicative strengths with Latin American and African cultures. However, the level of individual variation amongst parents and students would push most attempts at this linkage into assumptions at best, and stereotyping at worst.

Instead, this book recommends educators use this model to draw out strengths the parents themselves have observed, building a comprehensive model together. A curriculum that uses the strengths-based model can only be made effectively on a case-by-case basis. That being said, designing a curriculum template that is easily adaptable to different strengths can be useful, particularly when considering tweaking specific parts of lesson plans to fit the needs of larger classes. For example, a teacher might set up various learning stations in the classroom to allow all different types of students to learn in the way that suits them most. Another example is including flexibility in student projects.

Finally, educators may find that the different ways they design the classroom, specifically meant to adjust teaching methods for neurodiverse students, benefit the whole class. In this way, the strengths-based instruction model demonstrates the effectiveness of novel and unconventional teaching strategies throughout the greater system of education, showing that sticking to the standard pedagogical methods is not always best.

CREATIVITY IN TEACHER PEDAGOGY: DIFFERENTIATED INSTRUCTION

Differentiated instruction goes hand-in-hand with the strengths-based model of teaching. Together, these instruction models have the potential to transform the classroom into an inclusive place where all students can thrive. Combining the openness and flexibility of curriculum design in differentiated instruction and the focus on student strengths over deficits in the strengths-based model truly places student needs at the forefront of education. Focusing on student needs, particularly considering the neurological spectrum that widely diversifies student needs, ensures each individual student is given a real opportunity to succeed academically.

Quality differentiated instruction requires modifying core elements of teaching, including content, process, product, and effect. These elements derive from three areas of student needs, which vary from student to student: readiness, interest, and learning profile.[2] One way to think about how to modify instruction based on student needs is to adapt different aspects of teaching to variation between students.

For example, some students might struggle to listen to a teacher who talks and moves around simultaneously. Other students might have the reverse issue, where they have a hard time focusing on a teacher who sits still during instruction. In an environment where teachers must develop strategies not just for individual students but the whole class, having students with these two opposing learning types presents a problem. Awareness of the needs of neurodiverse students provides the opportunity to resolve the issue, whether that means being creative about instruction methods or seeking administrative support.

When communicating these differentiated methods to parents from different cultural backgrounds, particularly those with a more collectivist mindset, a useful tactic can be to make reference to how the methods were designed to assist other students. One educator working in Thai schools interviewed for this book noted that she always found it best to give all examples as related to other children and other success stories. She found that karma played a substantial role in the families' views toward disabilities, as they could be convinced immediately that a previous incident was reason for the current disability. By relating the observed neurodiverse characteristics and pedagogical interventions to other students "from her experience," this educator was able to impart necessary information without setting the parents on a path of shame or nihilism.

The substantial challenge around communications with families around neurodevelopmental disorders makes these experiences an optimal time to utilize the services of fellow educators from different backgrounds. One counselor interviewed for this book noted her work with a Pakistani family whose child had severe cognitive processing issues. From her perspective, the family was not ready for the level of work needed, instead seeking a "quick fix" for what they saw as primarily behavioral issues. The counselor engaged other colleagues from her school from similar cultural backgrounds to join the conversations, which helped to "hook" into parental values.

Ultimately, every parent wants to see their child safe and happy. Neurodiversity can be a frightening concept to introduce to parents from cultural backgrounds with low levels of understanding and acceptance of what differences naturally exist. Educators who are required to impart these messages to families should make full use of their empathic abilities, considering how the message may be received, and utilizing all available resources to move forward.

SUMMARY

Neurodiversity in the classroom can present a clear set of challenges for educators. Implementing strengths-based instruction together with differentiated instruction allows diverse learners to thrive, as these models prioritize student needs at the core of the curriculum design. Communications around neurodiversity with parents from different cultural backgrounds can be among the most difficult endeavors for any educator to undertake; each conversation requires understanding, empathy, and respect.

INTERACTIVE SELF-PRACTICE EXERCISES

1. Choose one cultural background that is well represented in your classroom. Consider how you would start a conversation about neurodiversity with families from that background, including what online resources you could make reference to.

2. Write out a list of students currently in your class. For each student, list their strengths according to the groupings in this chapter. Consider how you might alter your classroom dynamics and assignments to differentiate instruction amongst these strengths and convey these strengths to parents.

EFFECTIVE CONVERSATIONAL POINTS

With a colleague, discuss experiences working with students with neurodevelopmental disorders.

- How have these experiences made you a better teacher?
- How have these experiences made you a better person?
- What stories from these experiences might be valuable to share with families who might have little understanding of neurodiversity?

NOTES

1. Armstrong, T. (2013). *Neurodiversity in the Classroom: Strength-Based Strategies to Help Students with Special Needs Succeed in School and Life.* Alexandria, VA: ASCD.
2. van Geel, M., Keuning, T., Frerejean, J. et al. (2018). Capturing the complexity of differentiated instruction. *School Effectiveness and School Improvement: An International Journal of Research, Policy, and Practice* 30: 51–67. https://www.tandfonline.com/doi/full/10.1080/09243453.2018.1539013#:~:text.

PART IV

SUPPORTING STUDENTS WITH HIGHER EDUCATION PLANS

11

INTRODUCTION
TO SUPPORTING
STUDENTS WITH HIGHER
EDUCATION PLANS

Often, cultures reveal themselves in situations where much is at stake, like college admission. Interactions are shaped by deeply held cultural attitudes toward work, power, trust, wealth, and communication and can shape views on such things as ethics, grades and tests, extracurricular involvement, choosing a major, failure, mental health, relationships, socioeconomic factors, and family influence. The chapters in this part of the book are not meant to be a how-to guide for school/college counselors on the components of the admissions process, which would require its own dedicated space. The content is meant to support educators to better understand the various motivating and often complex factors parents and families may consider in making decisions about higher education.

It is also important to note that although school/high school admissions counseling is not directly discussed, much of the content here applies as the topics are about understanding how culture can impact perceptions. Although tips and sample scripts are provided, they should be used as general tools only as each situation is unique.

Additionally, "college" is not a term in some parts of the world (Canada, UK, etc.) to indicate higher ed institutions, but we will use the term "college counselor" and school, college, and university interchangeably in these chapters.

These chapters are for:

- Educators, administrators, or other professionals who mentor, support, and teach immigrant children and international students/families. Understanding the way families view the admissions processes or the reason to pursue higher education, which can be helpful in having thoughtful conversations with the parents when discussing student performance.

- High school/independent college counselors or Secondary Placement counselors working with immigrant families and international students/families whose students plan to pursue school/undergraduate education and are looking to gain culturally relevant information and guidance in talking with families of multicultural backgrounds.

OVERVIEW

Though not exclusive to this group, preparing immigrant and international students and families for the college admissions process takes careful preparation and time. A lack of knowledge about the religious needs, cultural concerns, and language barriers are just some of the obstacles families may need to overcome to ensure a smooth process.

In the admissions process, developing a college list can be a complicated process, in and of itself, but especially when working with families who come from multicultural backgrounds. Though the general ethos of college admissions preparation in the United States is one where the students take ownership, that some college counselors have mentioned it's one of the first major set of adult decisions they'd be making, this concept is simply not the case for many families, especially those from certain cultural backgrounds or outlooks whose cultural influences lead them to think the very opposite.

Calling back to the nuances of language and words, the idea of a "good" college may differ for everyone involved, including the student and counselors and even within a family. The term "good" is best avoided because it can imply that there is a set of colleges that are "good" and, therefore, there are some that are "bad," that may not have anything to do with what could make an institution "good" or "bad" (organized administration, generally satisfied staff and students, a generally safe and healthy environment, etc.) and thus propagate an unhealthy approach to the process.

It also distracts the focus away from "fit" and creates a system of arbitrary hierarchy, which is often influenced by various ranking lists that exist today that often are accepted without analysis or question. This can be dangerous for some, especially students and parents who may have high levels of anxiety. It can lead to an increased amount of pressure students feel from their parents, even if the parents consistently say school names are not important to them.

Attempts to get into the "top" or "good" schools, over the years, has caused a frenzy and mental health challenges of students and entire families, including grandparents and aunts and uncles, in some cultures. Many have associated their entire identity, self-worth, or others' self-worth and sometimes an entire family's value to society with the brand-name school. This road often ends with students who start to feel inadequate because within this approach, there's always someone better and you're told to be better than them, regardless of the multifaceted set of talents the students bring. For some students, rather than celebrating their unique self, they get anxious, depressed, and suicidal.

Such a value system—one defined by the brand-name school you attend and not one primarily based on kindness, character, and integrity—can shape students' views, especially during a critical identity development and value-assessment period.

The educator's repetitive redirecting to a healthier approach is essential just as in the same way the parents' understanding of how they discuss the process affects students sometimes more deeply than they are aware. That is, shooting for an Ivy League school is not the issue; the approach to how and why is more of the concern.

Chapters 12 and 13 will provide some insight into how some parents may view the process from a culturally influenced point of view and some ways to effectively discuss a healthier approach to the parents who often have the best intentions for their children.

12

NAVIGATING HIGH-PRESSURE CONSTRUCTS

Often parents are pressured themselves from their own respective societies, and as they want the best for their children, do not want their children to be on the sidelines. These "high stakes" can be reinforced by cultural values related to prestige as well as a higher tolerance for unequal distributions of power and resources.

This relation to "status" often surfaces in relation to competitive admissions for schools at the secondary or tertiary level and can be apparent particularly when stakeholders have an incomplete picture of the landscape of educational options. This cultural pressure often can be normalized through company recruiting practices as well as signals from political figures. In employment recruitment fairs in China, some companies state they will only accept résumés from graduates from one of the 50 highest-ranking universities in the QS World Ranking. Marina remembers having lunch with a former Korean Minister of Education during her graduate studies. He mentioned how proud he was that the two universities with the highest number of Koreans and Korean Americans were Harvard and Berkeley. This pride in "brand-name" universities would be difficult to imagine coming from a U.S. Secretary of Education given the lower power distance within mainstream American culture.

This pressure from the top quickly becomes internalized by students. Marina worked closely with "Mi Sook," a Korean student who went to a highly prestigious New England boarding school. Mi Sook was invited to a conference in Seoul for students studying abroad. Tables of students started to gather, many of whom wore sweatshirts with the names of the boarding school or college they attended.

Mi Sook was not wearing any identifying clothing and received a suspicious look when she approached one table. A girl asked her bluntly, "What school do you attend?"

Satisfied with Mi Sook's reply, the other girl continued, "That's a relief. We'd love to invite you to sit here. We're trying to keep this section reserved only for students who go to the top schools." Mi Sook sat down and started to engage with the group, seeing other students repeatedly turned away when their school didn't have the same recognition.

For many families and in our current society, there is a status stratification based on the school the child attends. Along with the feelings of pride, the prospect of a better job and higher pay can be essential for survival for many families, even beyond financial stability. For well-resourced international families, adding a global experience at the "right" school to a student's résumé is seen as a ready pathway to a better job. Additionally, prestigious schools are seen as a means for social mobility, a common pull factor for many immigrant families.

For some traditionally Confucian cultures, a "brand-name" education can have impact beyond the student. A child attending a prestigious university provides a signal that the family has performed their roles appropriately, and is deserving of an exalted status. The value of an adult's relationship to their children can be seen in language constructs, as many Korean parents will refer to themselves as "Harry's mom/dad." Oftentimes, they will "lose" their own given name, and only be known by their role in the family, reflecting the importance of this tie.

This is well illustrated in the case of the Korean figure skater Yuna Kim. Yuna became a national icon with an impressive record of finishing second at the 2004–2005 Junior Grand Prix Final, which earned Korea's first international medal. She had a tremendously successful career, capped by winning the gold medal at the 2010 Winter Olympics in Vancouver.[1] In the United States, biographies and autobiographies of such figures are common. However, in South Korea, a book about Yuna's mother became a national bestseller.[2]

As mentioned in previous chapters, in some collectivist-leaning cultures, the way a child performs reflects the entire family. This is their reality and their values that stem from hundreds of years of social imprinting. Thus, attending what they may value as a highly selective school in their society or family is of utmost importance.

Even the school list in and of itself is important, as it can offend parents and deflate a student's confidence completely if the "right" schools are not on the list. One way for educators to suggest "acceptable" schools is to start with the names the families may be the most familiar with, and of those, find the schools with different tiers of selectivity that may be the best fit. The following script may help set the stage for this conversation.

SCRIPT

First, ask in a questionnaire or discussion what students' definitions of "success" are and why. If they use words like, "get into a 'good' school," ask what makes up a good school and why those traits are important before asking what they are considering as good schools.

This is where many families may think you don't understand "their cultural value" if they need to explain something that's naturally assumed in their culture. This is where you could say, "We are familiar with the many reasons why this is important to you, but we found it helpful to the students if the parents can honestly articulate the why. We also found it healthier for the family to evaluate and critically analyze their own reasons."

This is something most families understand and it is a great way to help them see where their anxiety, if they have it, is coming from and evaluate the pressure on the students and whether it's worth it.

Although Korea and China have been mentioned as examples, mainly in the light of high academic standards, it is important to note that such experiences are not exclusive to these countries nor should they be categorized as ones who *only* care, if at all, about brand-name schools or prestige.

What it does do is show what's true of families, the parents love for and desire to want the best for their children whatever they have come to think is the best, and when speaking with parents, that's what should be kept in mind.

NOTES

1. Yuna Lee, Global Ambassador (n.d.). Special Olympics. https://www.specialolympics.org/about/ambassadors/yuna-kim.
2. Bourassa, S. (2014). An Olympic-sized empty nest: what will Yuna Kim's mom do now? *Today* Show (21 February). https://www.today.com/parents/olympic-sized-empty-nest-what-will-yuna-kims-mom-do-2d12146242.

13

CULTURAL
PERSPECTIVES
ON TESTING AND
CREATING
A COMPREHENSIVE
BEST-FIT COLLEGE LIST

Calling back to societies influenced by Confucius, for example, there is a significant importance placed on examinations. The Confucian examination system originally started during the Sui dynasty (581–618 CE) and fully developed during the Qing dynasty, some scholars note, and could be the reason for the school curriculum many Confucian-influenced societies have today.[1]

As mentioned in Chapter 4, those who passed the Imperial Palace (*jinshi*) examinations (the highest level after several local and regional examinations) became the most important people in China's educated class and became important members of the Chinese bureaucracy. Others who did not make it to this level or chose not to still held significant positions of leadership in their villages and became teachers, a highly respected position. Some scholars contend this civil service examination was an attempt to change to a more merit-based system—a way for even the poorest family to attain the ranks of the educated elite; it was often the main reason why people went to school in the first place. Doing all you can to attain high marks was, thus, important not only to oneself but for one's entire family; one can extrapolate how this system for social mobility is reflected today.

When Marina was working with a Colombian American student, the student, "Anne," received a 640 in her Verbal/English and an 800 in her Math section of the SAT I. Anne decided she was not going to retake the SAT as it was too difficult to prepare for, and she would rather focus her energy on other aspects of her life. Even though she was a straight A student and valedictorian in her class at an international school in Colombia, she came to terms with the fact that certain schools might not accept her based on the statistical admissions figures that showed students with the highest SAT scores and highest grades were the most admitted. Her parents supported her decision and hoped for the best.

When Anne received her acceptances, she was most excited about Brown University and Duke University, the two schools with programs that most appealed to her, despite their being very different environments (in curriculum, university culture, etc.). She got rejected from Harvard. She wasn't thrilled about it as she still hoped that Harvard would see past her scores (and she knew it was hard to say why she got rejected). After careful discussion with her family, she decided on Duke.

For a similar-in-profile Korean American student that same year, Su Ban, the idea of not taking another test would mean that she was not trying hard enough, not taking her life and career and academic attainment seriously, giving up, and thus was bringing some level of nuanced shame to her family. Su Ban worked even harder and asked her parents for more sessions with a tutor, and retook the SAT I, this time moving her Verbal/English score to a 760.

For many students in Korea, and especially many of those Confucian-influenced test-oriented societies, this is the norm; to pass up an opportunity to attend an Ivy League university, when all it takes is just to work a little harder, is uncommon. I mean, "Why not?" as one parent posed.

In Mexico and other Latin American countries, there is often a gender disparity that could be more common for the upper class. For boys, you can study one of five subjects: medicine, law, architecture, business, or engineering. If you're an artist, it's not uncommon to hear parents recommending architecture as the creative option. For girls, there's a sense that they'll stop working anyway as they're expected to get married and have children. Often in such cases, students may feel directed in a way that doesn't feel authentic to them.

Understanding the significant value on testing to move up in social mobility is still evident today in such cultures with this shared history. It's a good reminder to educators that often decisions that may seem like families are putting undue pressure on the children are coming from centuries of social norms that actually helped societies at the time to have order and opportunities for many. Though one could argue that such systems influenced a perverse approach to educational testing (heightened anxiety, value on self, especially regarding one's intelligence, or whether someone deserves to be in "good" schools, as some examples), as in the case with many Asian societies, Confucian values not only encourage knowledge but also integrity and character building, giving priority not to the individual but to the family, community, and world; his sayings are often quoted today by world leaders on peace, love, politics, and trustworthiness.[2]

CONCEPT OF SACRIFICE

Families from all cultures have worked hard to provide for their children in the best way they know how or with the situations that are presented to them, despite whether they succeed in trying to make the situation better.

One educator pointed out that in her work at an Ivy League institution as a dean and an advisor to students, she worked with "John," a student who was a second-generation immigrant from China. His family had made significant sacrifices (moving to a new country, long hours at work) to give him an education and pave the path for him to be an engineer, one of the acceptable career choices in some cultures. He did not want to go that route and felt enormous pressure from his parents to be something or someone he did not want to be.

John had fallen in love with history and though unsure of his career, knew analyzing history brought him significant joy. The fact that he wasn't as talented in math compared to some of his classmates made him feel inadequate, but in history, he thrived. His parents wanted him to work harder, asked his advisor at school to encourage him to do so, and followed up with his counselor about how they wanted him to apply to the most selective engineering schools. John keenly felt the burden of his parents' sacrifice—one he witnessed daily, seeing them work long hours to pay for his education—on his shoulders. He felt trapped, and, unfortunately, developed suicidal thoughts from this pressure.

Often in East Asian families, there's a general implicit understanding that the children are obligated to "pay back" their parents by finding their own joy and success. However, cultural values on prestige can cause this joy and success to be interpreted narrowly as needing to be one that leaves the next generation in a better position financially and the reputation of the family in higher social status.

In cases like this, some counselors have found it helpful to recognize that culture is also nuanced by socioeconomic status, race, ethnicity, location, etc., as well as other attributes of an individual. Useful tips can be:

- Recognize where the parents are coming from—for example, that they desire financial stability in their only child, that there's a sense the son will carry on their family line.
- Show and explicitly state that you are one team.
- List some college options where students can study both history and engineering, making sure there are some brand-names or recognizable schools on the list.
- Discuss how U.S. colleges are set up in a way where students can explore more disciplines and can change majors. Present statistics that show even when they do major in an academic discipline, most do not end up working in that field.
- Find statistics for successful careers for those with history knowledge that would classify as one of the acceptable careers, which mainly means medicine, law, engineering, finance, and business.

SAMPLE SCRIPT (Appendix 2 has some common greetings and gestures):

"Hello —.

(One common greeting in the Chinese style; shake their hand with your right, then cup the person's hand with your left and give a light bow. If they give you a business card, take it with both hands respectfully and look at both sides of the card. Put the card carefully in your wallet or on your desk if you don't have a safe place readily available.

The point of this exercise is to give a feeling of comfort to some parents who may especially feel lost in an English-speaking setting; for higher income/more affluent families, they may not appreciate it as much as they will pride themselves more in knowing English.)

"Thank you for coming in today to discuss your child's college process and options."

(Talk about things that are not confrontational briefly. The weather, celebrations coming up, etc.)

"We noticed you want a different set of schools on his list. I appreciate his interest in engineering. My main concern is that his heart doesn't seem to be in it. I understand though the need for that security that can be found in certain fields like engineering.

"We've also seen his talent in history, and he has a passion for it. We'd like to suggest that he applies to some colleges that have programs in both. This way, it'll be more helpful for him in his application and, more importantly, give a sense of control over this college process, which is important for students and their mental health. Plus, he'll have a higher chance of getting in. Don't worry. He'll still have a strong engineering/engineering-related option there, too."

(Suggest a few schools they may be somewhat familiar with. They're not necessarily looking for diversity of options but a list of familiar options, often found in ranking lists.)

As some cultures value the bosses more (e.g., many Asian countries), you may need the input from the school director, principal, or head to convince some families effectively.

It is important to note that when a student is applying to colleges in the UK, Canada, and United States the word "college" means something very different. In the UK, college is the two years before "uni," where the students prepare the university exams; it can also mean a technical school. In Canada, it does mean a technical school. In the United States, it is a university.

You become more credible in the parents' eyes when you use correct terminology. Not only are you trying to be sensitive culturally, you are knowledgeable. They may more likely believe what you say.

When college counselors support students to build a school list, many counselors would concur that many families (e.g., East Asian and some Southeast Asian, but not limited to those cultures), would have an unbalanced list or would want to apply to all the Ivy's or similar. Among many perceptions, often there could be a sense that the parents don't understand what it takes to get into these schools as well as that the parents aren't seeing their child in a realistic way. Educators may sense the parents are adding pressure to the child or only obsessed with rankings or brand names rather than what's a good fit for the child's development.

For many Latin American families, the concept of *enlaces familiares profundos, vinculos familiares*, or *lazos familiares*, meaning a profound connection to family and friends, runs deep, extending even from first to fifth cousins or distant friends. They often rely on each other or their friends on the names of a "good" school. For them, rather than necessarily looking at ranking, they may feel more comfortable with schools that a relative or someone they know went to, which is not the case for many Asians, speaking broadly.

For Arab families, there is a common phrase, *Al-ain mighrafet al-kalam*, which literally means "the eye is the spoon of speech." Seeing people when they are speaking is important, as a lot of nonverbal communications can be observed. When counselors discuss school lists or student performance and competitiveness for schools, showing them your face and being sincere will help them develop more trust in you.

Understanding such layers of sacrifice and significance to a college list can provide some context on building the right "fit" school list for families. It can be complicated. If not done well, the families may distrust the school/college counselor or think the counselor is unaware of the cultural elements and, therefore, has different values and is not reliable.

GENERAL VIEW OF ACCOUNTABILITY

Especially when the stakes feel so high, there can be a blame game when the students don't get into the "good" schools.

Some view the role of teachers/counselors as one to motivate the child: it's not my child's fault for not working hard enough or getting good grades and is not competitive enough now for college. It was the teachers' lack of providing inspiration or motivating the child that has caused this, calling back to the cultures who believe their obligations of roles. This is more common in collectivist societies.

Other countries may have a starkly opposite view. How my child performs is up to my child. The whole application process is in their hands, reflecting the American sense of individuality and independence and learning from mistakes.

This echoes research[3] that shows that Chinese parents see themselves as responsible for their children's successes and failures and believe that success is based on one's hard work. Support to this particular parent meant hand-holding the student throughout the process, helping choose schools, discussing essay topics, and helping move things along as efficiently as possible for and with the child. If you asked her, she would say that she was letting the child run the show, however. Her perception of support was within her own culturally influenced framework as the mother who should support the child's academic growth,[4] and echoed in "Parenting Attributions and Attitudes in Cross-Cultural Perspective" by Bornstein, Putnick, and Lansford,[5] but her child is writing the essays, asking their own questions, etc. This also calls back to individualistic versus collectivist cultures where the former values/traits considered "good" are autonomy, independence, and self-sufficiency.

In a college brainstorming session, as a part of an empathy exercise to help parents understand what students may go through when asked difficult soul-searching college essay questions, parents were asked what kind of descriptions they would write about themselves.

Many who came from an individualistic culture described themselves having traits that were mainly about them. Descriptions included, "I enjoy singing and like to think I have a sense of humor. Other parents write, "I try to be there for my husband and children, or I take care of my children." For the parent who felt the need to stand by the student's side, sometimes literally, during the admissions process, the parent sees themselves as a mother, a father, a grandmother, uncle, etc., first.

With many collectivist-influenced families, talking about accountability as "we" and "us" while still making clear your role as a counselor (that you do not influence admissions office, there are no negotiations, cannot guarantee acceptance, etc.) can be an effective way to show the "village" mentality but still clearly define your role. The team effort against all odds, whether or not the student is ultimately accepted, often will be appreciated.

Many parents of similar backgrounds echoed similar messages. However, not all parents from the same cultural background would behave the same way as this particular Chinese American mother had. It's important to note again that we shouldn't assume or judge that just because someone is from a certain cultural or racial background, then they *must* hold certain values and the different values are better or worse, necessarily.

What can be helpful is to set clear guidelines on your role, as some families are unsure what your role and responsibilities may be or the extent to which you have them.

- State your role: what you do and why. Have this available in different languages.
- Encourage parents/students to share information that can be helpful (divorce, unusual situation, illness). This can be a sensitive topic so it's been effective to say, "Some parents, though they weren't comfortable at first, shared that the family was going through a hostile divorce. Such information can be helpful in understanding certain behavioral patterns or application content of the student, and therefore be helpful."
- Be frank early on regarding competitiveness of college admissions, particularly for certain schools, so students have time to improve.

SCRIPT

"It's great to see you Mr./Mrs. X. I'm happy to answer questions you have. I thought I'd start out by saying more of my role and what I can do to support your child.

My role as a college counselor is . . . (say your responsibilities to set expectations, as doing so will help the parents manage expectations; some may have a different idea of what your role and responsibilities are; some examples are below).

- Offer advice on course selection during their time at school.

- Create career goals and plans.

- Meet three times throughout the year.

- Help build a college list by offering 20 to 30 schools based on the responses from the college questionnaire.

- Review essays two times over the summer but won't be making major edits.

- Write a counselor recommendation that consists of various teacher comments throughout the time the student has attended this school as well as from the college questionnaire responses (yours and students).

- I also advocate for your child by not only writing these recommendations but on occasion being on a call with admissions offices.

INTERACTIONS

Some may work at a school where the role of a college counselor is a guidance counselor, in which case the responsibilities may be broader.

Rather than rattling off a list of responsibilities, however, for the short period of time you have for a meeting, choose the most relevant ones related to the meeting. It often will be helpful for parents, in particular those who are literate, to have your list of responsibilities written down in multiple languages. Many have no idea school systems in the United States, for example, have such resources available for their students.

It is also highly recommended that concrete plans are also listed (meeting X number of times, be available beyond these times as often as needed, response time in the summer is one week, etc.). Distribute this list at the start of the school year and well before your first in-person meeting and let parents know you are available for questions.

On the same sheet with your responsibilities, list the expectations and roles students and parents play to better support the parents in the process, especially those who are unaware of your role.

For example, one could say:

"Generally, our office encourages students to . . ."

Research on their own a list of 20 to 30 schools we provide and choose which ones they like and why (show students how to do the research, especially if the students are used to different ways of approaching it based on experience from their previous country would be helpful; showing students what "flexible" or "research" means can be helpful as well).

> *"We encourage parents to support students to initiate and act on their own but to ask us questions when they need it."*

As in many cultures, taking initiative or asking questions can make parents feel they are bothering the teacher or being rude. It's important to acknowledge this. For example, you may say,

> *"I know you and your child(ren) always try to be so considerate and not bother me. I want to reassure you that you are not, and I prefer that I'm asked questions now and not have misunderstanding later."*

For cultures that may have a more collectivist idea toward education especially, you may want to say:

> *"We are a team working together to support your child through a complicated process."*

For some families coming from a culture where there's a sense that it's mainly your responsibility and not the child's to complete the process successfully, you may want to say:

> *"Your child is the main person on the team and we're supporters. We can all guide your child on which direction to take, but it will ultimately need to be your child who wants to receive the guidance."*

Questions to ask parents:
- This is a question for more of the affluent families of certain cultures, though not limited to them: What are your expectations of me as the college counselor/guidance counselor? What role do you plan to play, if you have an idea now, in the admissions process?
  - Some parents will have no idea and will defer to you, each though with different reasons. Some because they honestly have no idea, and if they knew, they would be more involved; in some cultures, they may defer to you because teachers are the ones who are supposed to guide the student's educational pursuits and not the parents, especially when it comes to college admissions or pedagogical issues. You would often hear,

"You're the teacher; whatever you think is best," that also implies "You should be making the decisions. Why are you asking me?" Some of this may be reflected more in the Singaporean, Turkish, South Korean, and Malaysian cultures.

- As I advocate for your child, it might also help if you can share anything that has had a personal impact on the children, including divorce, separation, a difficult situation, etc., only if you feel comfortable.

  - You might want to add in a couple short anecdotes so they can see this is a norm. For example, there was a family Marina worked with who was going through a hostile divorce. This impacted the children in ways that was confusing to teachers in that the girls always looked tired after the weekend. They traveled six hours every weekend to see their father and sometimes came back late at night on Sunday/early morning on Monday. You could give such an anecdote and say that "because the teacher knew this, he made slight adjustments to the weekend homework for all the students." This gives a sense to the parents that there was no backlash. This could help some cultures that are generally more private like the Ukrainian or Russian.

- For the more affluent families in certain cultures, like those of Latin America, there could be a misunderstanding that money can buy paths in to opportunities, as it does in their country. They may ask how much it would cost to have the student attend a certain school. It would be good here to emphasize that there is no shortcut to admissions.

When giving feedback about student performance as it relates to college applications, it's best to focus on the facts. Many parents want facts and anything less than an A is not "good" when discussing the grades.

When Marina was speaking with a Russian immigrant parent and a Chinese immigrant parent one week, both of whom had parent-teacher conferences that week, they both said how the students are doing great and were happy with the meeting. The teachers seemed generally happy with the progress of the students. Marina asked them to follow up with the teacher to find out about the grades for the class. They were both surprised each of their children were earning a B. They were confused at why the teacher would say that their child was doing great. If they had known earlier, they would have talked with the student. At that point, they thought the students had ruined their chances for a highly selective school.

RECOMMENDATION LETTERS

Finally, when writing recommendation letters, it's important to be aware of your own biases. For example, one college counselor realized he described most Asian students as "diligent and hard-working," and male students as "analytical" and female students as "sweet." Though this may be true, it's beneficial to see if other non-Asian students had similar descriptions, as surely, there were many non-Asian students who would have such traits. In another rec-ommendation letter, a well-meaning teacher wrote, "I was impressed with the student's work; especially for an Asian, I found his active role and leadership in difficult discussions helpful for the class."

In another example, two teachers commented on each other's letters, pointing out the biases they read in the other's recommendation letters.

For example, one of the letters read, "Victoria is an adopted Vietnamese student and often confided in me about her relationship with her Asian culture. I was impressed with her confidence in shedding her Vietnamese side. The decision to do so is a sign of maturity that comes from deeper self-reflection of self."

As the teacher who was Asian pointed out to the other, shedding your racial ties is not an option and certainly not a sign of maturity or deep reflection. No matter where Victoria goes, she will always be seen as Asian. Not accepting this side of her will cause some signifi-cant challenges in her life.

When educators write recommendation letters, it could be helpful to ask a colleague to look out for implicit biases not only for the educator's professional development but also to best support students.

SUMMARY

No matter the cultural background of the family, the college admissions process can be highly stressful. Some families perceive a higher stake in the outcome than others, and it can be important to identify who is in the network of counseling and making decisions for each student. For some, this network can be vast. When working with the grandchild of the founder of one of the largest corporations in Asia, Marina found that the parents, the grand-parents, and, to some extent, all of the company were a part of the evaluating his college prospects and choices.

To move forward with integrity requires creating trust with the students and families, and also encouraging healthy mindsets around potential pathways forward. During Marina's 25 years of experience working with students and families of various backgrounds, kindness and authenticity are the ultimate lodestones for admissions counseling with families.

In 2016, Professor Richard Weissbourd, in collaboration with Lloyd Thacker, Director of The Education Conservancy, with the input of college admissions deans and other stake-holders in the college admissions process, wrote *Turning the Tide*.

An offshoot of the Harvard Graduate School of Education's Making Caring Common project, the purpose was to reshape the existing college admissions process to one where the focus is not on grades but on care and contribution to our communities. We strongly recommend reading *Turning the Tide* and utilizing the Making Caring Common curriculum, which supports educators, parents, and communities to raise children as responsible and caring citizens to their communities.[6]

SELF-PRACTICE EXERCISES FOR EDUCATORS

1. Imagine your child is studying in a country you are not familiar with. What are some concerns you will have? What information would you rely on? What if someone tells you the information you're reading is incorrect? What do you wish your child's counselor/teacher knew about your family/child?

    (a) How does your cultural identity influence your daily actions and perceptions? How does your cultural knowledge/assumptions influence decision-making in the college process? In what ways and why?

    (b) What cultural considerations should the counselor be sensitive to in discussion with this student and family?

2. What other considerations should the counselor be mindful of?

3. How will you relay relevant school information to parents?

4. To what extent will you relay what was said to you in private to the parents?

5. What are the skills that will support you in working effectively across cultures?

6. What is your level of understanding about the culture of individuals you engage with?

7. How do you manage your own bias?

8. What are two ways you can help redirect anxiety-causing stressful conversations to one where students can learn more about themselves? To understand the importance of strong contributions to the community, not for the sake of being admitted?

COLLEGE ADMISSIONS RESOURCES

- Step by step: college awareness and planning for families, counselors, and communities: https://www.nacacnet.org/advocacy.
- Pathways to College: pathwaystocollege.org.
- Education USA: educationusa.state.gov.
- WES Global Talent Bridge: https://www.wes.org/partners/global-talent-bridge/.
- ESL Tool Kit, Pathways to Success Seminars: https://lincs.ed.gov/professional-development/resource-collections/profile-722.

- WES Advisor: https://wes.org/advisor-blog/.
- Degree Equivalency applications: https://applications.wes.org/degree-equivalency-tool/.
- iGPA Calculator applications: https://applications.wes.org/igpa-calculator/.
- Dimensions of Culture by the U.S. State Department, "So You're an American: A Guide to Answering Difficult Questions Abroad": https://www.state.gov/courses/answeringdifficultquestions/html/app.htm?p=module1_p1.htm.

NOTES

1. Living in the Chinese Cosmos. (n.d.). The Confucian classics & the civil service examinations. http://afe.easia.columbia.edu/cosmos/irc/classics.htm.
2. Wen, Y. (2014). Confucianism and its influence today. ChinaCulture.org (10 October). http://en.chinaculture.org/focus/2014-10/10/content_567522.htm.
3. Bornstein, M.H., Putnick, D.L., and Lansford, J.E. (2011). Parenting attributions and attitudes in cross-cultural perspective. *Parenting Science and Practice* 11 (2-3): 214–237. https://www.ncbi.nlm.nih.gov/pmc/articles/PMC3173779/ (accessed 2 October 2022).
4. Ibid; research also shows this.
5. Ibid.
6. Harvard Graduate School of Education. (2016). Turning the tide: Inspiring concern for others and the common good through college admissions. Press release (20 January). https://www.gse.harvard.edu/news/16/01/turning-tide-inspiring-concern-others-and-common-good-through-college-admissions; Making Caring Common Project. (2016). Turning the tide: Inspiring concern for others and the common good through college admissions. Harvard Graduate School of Education (January). https://mcc.gse.harvard.edu/reports/turning-the-tide-college-admissions; Making Caring Common Project. (n.d.). Character assessment in college admission guide overview. Harvard Graduate School of Education https://mcc.gse.harvard.edu/resources-for-colleges/character-assessment-college-admission-guide-overview.

Appendix 1

LEARNING THROUGH EXTRACURRICULAR ACTIVITIES

Often many immigrant families who lack social and cultural capital do not know about the school offerings and/or the learning that can happen within them.

Below are three extracurricular activities examples with their learning points in English, Spanish, and Chinese.

ENGLISH

For all extracurricular activities below, learning points can be:

- Create opportunity to connect with peers who have similar interests/passions.
- Become part of a community.
- Develop a sense of belonging.
- Increased confidence/boost self-esteem.

Debate Team/Mock Trial/Model UN

- Practice public speaking and research skills.
- Learn to articulate/communicate your ideas effectively with words.
- Learn to control your emotions/stay calm in high-pressure situations.
- Learn to listen carefully to opponents' points for successful refutation.
- Learn how to state your case/argue effectively for an idea.

Student Council/Student Government

- Learn to collaborate and communicate effectively with others—gain "soft skills."
- Practice leadership skills.
- Give back to your community.
- Learn how to be an advocate for a greater cause and everyone in your community.
- It is easy to complain about what one thinks is wrong, but as a student leader one learns how difficult it really is to achieve systematic change and all the effort that it really requires, not just from the students but all parties involved.

School Newspaper

- Develop writing/design/business/leadership skills → depending on the section of the newspaper (sales, administration, accounting), students gain valuable experience for a future in journalism and many other fields.
- Learn to take on responsibility, manage your time, and partially work on other people's schedules because for the final product (newspaper) to be created, everyone's contribution is required at a specific deadline.
- Learn more about your campus/community.

Community Service Clubs

- Engage in your community and leave a positive impact.
- Gain understanding of other ways of life.
- Raise social awareness.
- Could possibly make students more interested in social justice.
- Create a sense of purpose.
- Practice gratitude.
- Reduce stress.

Academic Subject Clubs

- Dive deeper into a subject you are passionate about.
- Meet likeminded students who share similar interests → can learn a lot from each other.
- Join competitions (Science Olympiad, AMC, etc.).
- Educate your community on a certain subject.
- Opportunity for networking.

Language Clubs

- Improve language skills in an environment where you are constantly surrounded by the language.
- Put your knowledge into practice outside of the formality and structure of the classroom.
- Practice a foreign language.
- Stay in touch with your native language.
- Learn more about the cultures from the countries in which your language is spoken.

Peer Tutoring

- Gain a new perspective on teaching, learning, and education in general.
- Tutors learn to be patient while explaining and use creative ways to explain something.
- Strengthen their understanding of a subject.

Musical/Plays

- Increase confidence performing/speaking in front of a large audience.
- Improve time management skills and how to prioritize tasks (rehearsals can last hours after a long day of school or take up an entire weekend in the weeks leading up to a performance).
- Learn that there is always room for improvement—unlike on a test where scoring 100% is the best a student can perform, there is no such thing as perfection in the performing arts.
- Learn to take criticism—not everyone in the audience will enjoy your craft, just like how not everyone in life will like you, and that is a reality students must come to terms with and not take personally.
- Develop empathy—not everyone will relate to their characters on a personal level, but it is important to learn to understand them to be able to perform them authentically.

Sports Teams

- Physical movement improves general health and academic performance.
- Learn to collaborate effectively in teams to work toward a common goal.
- Improve critical-thinking and problem-solving skills—athletes must think quick on their feet when playing against an unfamiliar opponent.
- Learn the lesson that life isn't always fair—for example, when a wrong penalty is called, students must learn to accept it and move on.
- Learn to accept defeat—you win as a team and you lose as a team.
- Teach discipline—training can be extremely rigorous, and as a team each member has to pull their weight.

SPANISH

Para todas las actividades

- La oportunidad de conectarse con compañeros que tienen intereses/pasiones similares.
- La parte de una comunidad.
- Desarrollar un sentido de pertenencia.
- Aumento de confianza/ aumenta a la autoestima.

Equipo de debate/simulacro de juicio/Modelo ONU

- Practicar hablar en público y habilidades de investigación.
- Aprender a articular/comunicar sus ideas con palabras.
- Aprender a controlar sus emociones/mantener la calma en situaciones de alta presión.
- Aprender a escuchar atentamente a los puntos de los oponentes para una refutación exitosa.
- Aprender cómo exponer su caso/argumentar una idea efectivamente.

Consejo Estudiantil/Gobierno Estudiantil

- Aprender a colaborar y comunicarse de manera efectiva con los demás: adquirir "habilidades blandas."
- Practicar habilidades de liderazgo.
- Devolver a la comunidad.
- Aprender a ser un defensor de una causa mayor y de todos en su comunidad.
- Es fácil quejarse de lo que uno piensa que está mal, pero como líder estudiantil, se aprende lo difícil que es realmente lograr el cambio sistemático y todo el esfuerzo que realmente requiere, no solo de los estudiantes, pero de todos los partidos involucrados.

Periódico escolar

- Desarrollar habilidades de escritura/diseño/negocios/liderazgo → depende de la sección del periódico (ventas, administración, contabilidad), los estudiantes adquieren experiencia valiosa para un futuro en el periodismo y muchos otros campos.

- Aprender a asumir responsabilidades, administrar su tiempo y trabajar con los horarios de los demás, porque para crear el producto final (el periódico), se requiere la contribución de todos en un plazo específico.

- Aprender más de su campus/comunidad.

Clubes de servicio comunitario

- Participar en la comunidad y dejar un impacto positivo.

- Adquirir comprensión de otras formas de vida.

- Aumenta la conciencia social.

- Podría hacer que los estudiantes se interesen más en la justicia social.

- Crear un sentido de propósito.

- Practicar la gratitud.

- Reducir el estrés.

Clubes de materias académicas

- Profundizar en un tema que te apasione.

- Conocer a estudiantes con idea afines que comparten intereses similares → pueden aprender mucho unos de otros.

- Participar en competiciones (Olimpiada de Ciencias, AMC, etc.).

- Educar a su comunidad sobre un tema determinado.

- Oportunidades para hacer networking.

Clubes de idiomas

- Mejorar sus habilidades lingüísticas en un entorno en que está constantemente rodeado por el idioma.

- Poner en práctica sus conocimientos fuera de la formalidad y estructura del aula.

- Practicar un idioma extranjero.

- Mantenerse en contacto con su lengua nativa.

- Aprender más sobre las culturas de los países en que se habla su idioma de estudios.

Tutoría de iguales

- Obtener una perspectiva nueva sobre la enseñanza, el aprendizaje, y la educación en general.
- Los tutores aprenden a ser pacientes mientras explican y usan maneras creativas para explicar algo.
- Fortalecer su comprensión de un tema.

Musicales/Obras de Teatro

- Aumentar la confianza al actuar/hablar frente a una gran audiencia.
- Mejorar las habilidades de gestión del tiempo y cómo priorizar funciones (los ensayos pueden durar horas después de un largo día o tomar todo un fin de semana de las semanas previas a una actuación).
- Aprender que siempre hay espacio para mejorar—a diferencia de una prueba en que sacar un 100% es lo mejor que puede hacer un estudiante- no existe la perfección en las artes escénicas.
- Aprender a aceptar las críticas—no todos en la audiencia se van a disfrutar de su oficio, al igual que no les cae bien a todos en la vida, y esa es una realidad que no los estudiantes deben aceptar y no tomar personalmente.
- Desarrollar la empatía—no todos se van a identificar con sus personajes a nivel personal, pero es importante aprender a comprenderlos para poder interpretarlos con autenticidad.

Equipos deportivos

- El movimiento físico mejora la salud general y el rendimiento académico.
- Aprender a colaborar efectivamente en equipos para trabajar hacía un meta común.
- Mejorar las habilidades de pensamiento crítico y resolución de problemas—los atletas deben pensar rápido cuando juegan contra un oponente desconocido.
- Aprender la lección que la vida no siempre es justa- por ejemplo, cuando sanciona una penalización equivocada, los estudiantes deben aprender a aceptarla y seguir adelante.
- Aprender a aceptar la derrota: gana como equipo y pierde como equipo.
- Enseñar la disciplina- el entrenamiento puede ser extremadamente riguroso y como equipo cada miembro tiene que esforzarse.

CHINESE

Extracurricular activities	Purpose	Key takeaways	Learning points
国家荣誉项目活动	增加社会责任感，为成为世界公民做出准备。	国家荣誉项目证书，学习关于当今社会的知识，交到更多朋友。	沟通能力 合作能力 组织能力 时间管理能力 审辩性批判性思维能力
辩论组、法庭模拟、小小联合国	学生以准备、参与辩论会去了解社会现象的两面性。	通过辩论能学到大量关于课题本身的知识，同时也可以去辩证的去看待一个现象或者事物。	合作能力 时间管理能力 研究能力 逻辑能力
学生会	学生将在组织学校活动和帮助校方考虑学校全面发展的事务中成为主要角色。	学生能够和学生会成员们一起去组织、管理、参与多种学校活动。学生会领导还会从中获得更多去思考问题、计划方案的能力。	组织能力 沟通能力 体能(如果要去做体力活的话) 头脑风暴(想象力) 领导力
管弦乐团&乐队&合奏	学生会成为一场音乐演出的一员。通过练习自身擅长的音乐能力(乐器、歌唱)以在学校音乐会或其他公开活动中表演。	学生会在乐队里获得更多练习自己音乐演奏水平的机会。他们还可以通过每一次表演学会一首曲子的演奏方式(歌词、旋律)等。对于类似IB等部分教育体系中，音乐演奏会给予他们课业上的学分。	音乐演奏能力 合作能力 时间管理能力
合唱团&音乐剧	学生们会在每一次表演中按照指示来歌唱自己的声部，并且反复合作练习去唱好一首歌。学生们还会在导演的领导下在音乐剧中扮演属于自己的角色，以提高自身对于角色和戏剧的理解。	学生们会反复练习多首歌曲和戏剧的动作。他们会从中提高自身演技、歌唱技巧和记忆曲谱和台词的能力。他们还会在这些活动中交到更多朋友。	歌唱技巧 戏剧动作技巧 记忆能力 合作能力

(Continued)

Extracurricular activities	Purpose	Key takeaways	Learning points
舞台&化妆后勤	学生们将投入对每一场表演或活动的化妆、前期工作和后期工作，担任核心角色，为保证每一次活动都能顺利举行	学生们将会通过后勤体会劳动的感觉。他们也会通过相应指示从中学到一些前期准备工作、化妆和清扫工作的必要技能	体能 化妆技巧 合作能力
社会服务社团	学生们将参与附近社区的活动并提供诸如慈善活动和社会帮助等工作。主要为助于学生提高自身社会责任感，使他们更了解学校之外的社会现实	学生将能够理解一个社区的社会生活全貌。他们还能通过一些特殊人群来学到一些知识，例如需要接受特殊教育的人们在特殊教育之下的人们。学生们还会去学习如何去合作组织活动以及如何去和不同社区的重要人员去沟通以决定开始一项社会活动。	合作能力 沟通能力 领导能力 认知能力 组织能力 观察能力
学科社团	学生们会在某一学科社团中去探寻更广更深层次的知识。	学生们会通过社团去在某一学科上学到更多知识。他们也有能力将知识应用到现实生活中。他们也将能够去将知识进行实际运用。学生们也可能靠参与社团的活动去提高自己的成绩。	认知能力 审辩性批判性思维能力
语言社团	学生们会在(对自己来说)外语社团去练习他们的口头表达能力。他们也会收到对于语言运用的熟练度的反馈。	学生们会在互相交流中提高自己的口语能力。他们也会从中和不同语言及文化背景的人交友。	沟通能力 认知能力
精神&心灵社团	学生们会参与多种有助于心理健康的活动以减少来自每天大量课业带来的压力，以保证学生们知道如何在一天的劳累后放松自己。	学生们会学习诸如瑜伽等放松心灵的活动动作。他们也会学到在压力之下如何去放松。	体能 自我控制(心理)能力

Appendix 2

COMMON GREETINGS

Common Greetings and Gestures

Country	Some Common Ways of Greeting	Details
Argentina	A hug and kiss on the cheek; Handshake	Male, female, old, young, it doesn't matter: Whether you want one or not, you're getting a hug and a kiss on the cheek. For professional situations, you should give a firm handshake with direct eye contact and a welcoming smile.
Australia	Right-handed handshakes	Right-handed handshakes are customary in Australia and should be accompanied by direct eye-contact.
Brazil	Kiss on the cheek one to three times; Handshake	Depending on the region, you'll kiss one to three times; however, the single ladies tend to give an extra smooch. For professional greetings, the most common and appropriate greeting for anyone is a handshake. In Brazil, handshakes are usually firm, although some may prefer lighter handshakes. Brazilians usually take the time to greet each person individually, making direct eye contact. *(Continued)*

Country	Some Common Ways of Greeting	Details
China (including Hong Kong)	Bow or shake hands	In formal settings, the Chinese bow is common. But in recent years, handshakes have become the norm. In business, deference is always given to the oldest member of a group as they will be the one in the most senior position. Bowing or shaking hands are accepted forms of welcome. In Hong Kong, where both English and Chinese cultures have combined over the years, a light handshake, with lowered eyes as a mark of respect, is typical for business. There is no need for the additional bowing that is present in other Asian cultures.
France	Kiss on the cheeks three or four times; Handshake	In France the cheek-to-cheek—or cheek-to-cheek-to-cheek—kiss is as regional as the country's wines. In Paris, the standard is two. The more professional greeting is a handshake. French-style handshakes are known to be brisk and light. You should expect a loose grip with only one or two up and down movements.
Germany	A firm handshake	It's best to shake everyone's hand upon entering and exiting a meeting and not to shake someone's hand with one hand still in your pocket. Also, maintain eye contact.
Greece	A kiss and a slap on the back; Handshake	Greeks tend to give two kisses to ease the pain of the slap on the back. People usually are addressed by their appropriate title, e.g., *Keerios* (Mr.) for men and *Keeria* (Mrs.) for women. Some address elders who are not related as *Theia* (Aunty) and *Theios* (Uncle). For professional greeting, shaking hands is the most typical way, maintaining direct eye contact.

Country	Some Common Ways of Greeting	Details
India	Place palms together and say Namaste; Handshake	Place your palms together like a prayer, tilt your head forward, and say *Namaste*, which means, "adoration to you." As with the social structure in India, there is a formal hierarchical system that pervades business dealings. Personal space is important. Therefore, maintaining a gap of an arm's length between you and the other person is important. In business, handshakes are now more common. Indian women may not shake hands with men; Western women should also wait for Indian men to extend their hands.
Italy	Kiss on each cheek; Firm handshake	A quick kiss on each cheek—usually right, then left (your left, then your right). Most of the time, it's common to brush cheeks and make a kissing sound. The common greeting is a handshake with direct eye contact and a smile. If the greeting is between a man and a woman, the woman generally extends her hand first. It is common to give air kisses on both cheeks (starting with your left) when greeting those you know well. This is called the *il bacetto*. However, in Southern Italy, men generally only kiss family members and prefer to give a pat on the back to show affection in a greeting.
Japan	Bow	The bow is the standard greeting in Japan. Depending on the formalities, bows differ in duration, declination, and style. Among peers, the bow may be subtle. How far to bow depends on the relationship and status of the individuals bowing—the lower you bow the more respect you show. A slight bow of the head is generally acceptable for foreign visitors.

(Continued)

Country	Some Common Ways of Greeting	Details
Mexico	Handshake	Most initial introductions are accompanied by a handshake but may progress to a hug or a back slap (among men) and a touch on the right arm or shoulder for women.
Portugal	Kiss on each cheek; Firm handshake	It is appropriate to shake hands with everyone present in formal situations.
Russia	Handshake	A very firm handshake is the typical greeting among men in Russia, accompanied by direct eye contact. But when shaking hands with women, this handshake is much less firm.
South Korea	Bow accompanied by a handshake	In South Korea, the traditional greeting is a bow, which is often accompanied by a handshake for men that involves supporting your right forearm with your left hand while shaking. Korean women don't often shake hands but tend to nod instead of bowing.
Spain	Kiss on each cheek; Firm handshake	A firm handshake with eye contact and a smile is the appropriate greeting in a professional context.
Thailand	Press hands together and slightly bow	There's only one correct way greet in Thailand, and that's to press your hands together in a prayer-like fashion and slightly bow to your acquaintance.
The Netherlands, Belgium, and Switzerland	Kiss the cheeks three times from the right to left to right (your left to right to left); Handshake	For nonprofessional greetings, vague acquaintances stick to handshakes and uncomfortable silence. For these countries' professional greetings, it's typical to shake hands. Handshakes are firm with eye contact.
The United Kingdom	Handshake	A handshake, preferably with little eye contact and some light incoherent mumbling, is ideal in Britain.

Country	Some Common Ways of Greeting	Details
United Arab Emirates and Saudi Arabia	Touch noses; Handshake	In the UAE, Saudi Arabia, and a number of Persian Gulf countries, the go-to greeting isn't a handshake or kiss on the cheek, but rather it's touching noses. Formality and respect are very important in the UAE and are linked to the Islamic religion, which demands modest dress. No public displays of affection between the opposite sexes, with high regard for religion and the ruling elites. For professional greetings, a light handshake is the most typical form (males/females should not touch) or the right hand placed flat over your heart with a slight bow and can be accompanied by the term *Hayyakum*, which means hello/welcome.
United States	Handshake; Fist bump; Hug; Wave	There's the handshake, fist bump (Thanks, Obama), hug, bro-hug, "the nod," and the ever-endearing half-excited wave. A handshake is the most common greeting when meeting someone for the first time or in professional settings. Handshakes should be firm and accompanied with direct eye contact throughout the greeting, especially in business contexts.

RESOURCES CONSULTED

Blue Beyond Consultants. (n.d). 6 tips for effective leadership communication in a diverse workplace. https://www.bluebeyondconsulting.com/thought-leadership/6-tips-effective-leadership-communication-diverse-workplace/.

Agostinelli, F., Doepke, M., Sorrenti, G., and Zilibotti, F. (2020). It takes a village: the economics of parenting with neighborhood and peer effects. National Bureau of Economic Research working paper 27050.

Alampay, L.P. and Jocson, R.M. (2011). Attributions and attitudes of mothers and fathers in the Philippines. *Parenting: Science and Practice* 11 (2–3): 163–176. https://www.ncbi.nlm.nih.gov/pmc/articles/PMC3150789/.

Alta California Regional Center. (n.d.). Understanding Slavic Culture: Cultural Differences. https://www.altaregional.org/sites/main/files/file-attachments/cultural_differences10.18_slavic_culture.pdf?1597350164#:~:text.

Ambler, P. G., Eidels, A., and Gregory, C. (2015). Anxiety and aggression in adolescents with autism spectrum disorders attending mainstream schools. Research in Autism Spectrum Disorders 18: 97–109. https://www.sciencedirect.com/science/article/abs/pii/S1750946715000938.

American Psychological Association. (2009). APA concise dictionary of psychology. Washington, DC: American Psychological Association.

Barnes, T.N. and McCallops, K. (2019). Perceptions of culturally responsive pedagogy in teaching SEL. *Journal for Multicultural Education*, 13(1), 70–81.

Baron-Cohen, S. (2019). The concept of neurodiversity is dividing the autism community. *Scientific American* (30 April). https://blogs.scientificamerican.com/observations/the-concept-of-neurodiversity-is-dividing-the-autism-community/.

Beck J.S. (2005). *Cognitive Therapy for Challenging Problems*. New York: Guilford Press.

Bejanyan, K., Marshall, T.C., and Ferenczi, N. (2015). Associations of collectivism with relationship commitment, passion, and mate preferences: opposing roles of parental influence and family allocentrism. PLoS One (26 February).

Bianchi, E.C. (2016). American individualism rises and falls with the economy: cross-temporal evidence that individualism declines when the economy falters. *Journal of Personality and Social Psychology* 111 (4): 567–584. doi:10.1037/pspp0000114.

Blume, H. (1997). "Autism & the Internet" or "It's the Wiring, Stupid." Media in Transition (1 July). http://web.mit.edu/m-i-t/articles/index_blume.html.

Burnham, K. (2020). 5 culturally responsive teaching strategies. Northeastern University Graduate Programs Blog (31 July). https://www.northeastern.edu/graduate/blog/culturally-responsive-teaching-strategies/ (accessed 13 March 2022).

Callegari, C., Ielmini, M., Caselli, I. et al. (2019). The 6-D Model of National Culture as a Tool to Examine Cultural Interpretation of Migration Trauma-Related Dissociative Disorder: A Case Series. *Journal of Immigrant and Minority Health* 22: 588–596, table 6. https://link.springer.com/article/10.1007/s10903-019-00904-7/tables/6.

Calzada, E.J. (2010). Bringing culture into parent training with Latinos. *Cognitive and Behavioral Practice* 17 (2): 167–175. https://www.ncbi.nlm.nih.gov/pmc/articles/PMC4422064/.

Carrascosa-Romero, M.C., Vega, C.D., and La, C.D. (2015). The comorbidity of ADHD and autism spectrum disorders (ASDs) in community preschoolers. In: *ADHD: New Directions in Diagnosis and Treatment* (ed. J.M. Norvilitis), 109–164. London: IntechOpen. https://cdn.intechopen.com/pdfs-wm/49117.pdf.

Living in the Chinese Cosmos. (n.d.). The Confucian Classics & the Civil Service Examinations. Columbia University. Asia for Educators. http://afe.easia.columbia.edu/cosmos/irc/classics.htm (accessed 13 March 2022).

Conrad, P. and Bergey, M.R. (2014). The impending globalization of ADHD: notes on the expansion and growth of a medicalized disorder. *Social Science & Medicine* 122: 31–43.

Cross, T.L. (2003). Culture as a resource for mental health. *Cultural Diversity and Ethnic Minority Psychology* 9 (4): 354–359.

Evason, N. (2018). Mexican culture. Cultural Atlas. https://culturalatlas.sbs.com.au/mexican-culture/mexican-culture-core-concepts.

Day-Vines, N.L., Wood, S.M., Grothaus, T. et al. (2007). Broaching the subjects of race, ethnicity, and culture during the counseling process. *Journal of Counseling & Development* 85: 401–409.

Demeneix, B. (2014). *Losing Our Minds: How Environmental Pollution Impairs Human Intelligence and Mental Health*. New York: Oxford University Press. https://www.researchgate.net/publication/264905260_Losing_our_Minds_How_Environmental_Pollution_Impairs_Human_Intelligence_and_Mental_Health_Barbara_Demeneix_From_the_Oxford_Series_in_Behavioral_Neuroendocrinology.

DiGiacomo, D.K. and Gutiérrez, K.D. (2017). Seven chilis: making visible the complexities in leveraging cultural repertoires of practice in a designed teaching and learning environment. *Pedagogies: An International Journal* 12 (1): 41–57.

The Coca-Cola Company. (n.d.). Diversity, Equity & Inclusion. https://www.coca-colacompany.com/shared-future/diversity-and-inclusion.

Dupoux, E., Hammond, H., Ingalls, L., and Wolman, C. (2006). Teachers' attitudes toward students with disabilities in Haiti. *International Journal of Special Education* 21 (3): 1–14. https://www.researchgate.net/publication/285962893_Teachers%27_attitudes_toward_students_with_disabilities_in_Haiti.

Fitzgerald, T.K. (1997). Understanding diversity in the workplace: cultural metaphors or metaphors of identity? *Business Horizons* 40 (4): 66–70. https://www.sciencedirect.com/science/article/abs/pii/S0007681397900410.

Froehlich, J. and Nesbit, S. (2004). The aware communicator: dialogues on diversity. *Occupational Therapy in Health Care* 18 (1): 171–184. https://doi.org/10.1300/j003v18n01_16.

Gerdeman, D. (2017). Minorities who "whiten" job resumes get more interviews. (2017). Harvard Business School Working Knowledge (17 May). https://hbswk.hbs.edu/item/minorities-who-whiten-job-resumes-get-more-interviews.

Goodman-Scott, E., Hays, D.G., and Cholewa, B.E. (2018). "It takes a village": a case study of positive behavioral interventions and supports implementation in an exemplary urban middle school. *The Urban Review* 50 (1): 97–122.

Graham-Clay, S. (n.d.). Communicating with parents: strategies for teachers. *The School Community Journal* 117–129. https://www.adi.org/journal/ss05/graham-clay.pdf.

Hajin, L.Y. (2016). [Korean culture 101] When "no" actually doesn't mean "no." *The Korea Daily* (3 February). https://www.koreadailyus.com/korean-culture-101-accepting-compliments/.

Harb, C. (2016). The Arab region: cultures, values, and identities. In: *Handbook of Arab American Psychology* (eds. M. Amer and G. Awad). New York: Routldge. https://www.researchgate.net/publication/319159856_The_Arab_Region_Cultures_Values_and_Identities.

Herrera, D.R. (2015). The Philippines: an overview of the colonial era. *Southeast Asia in the Humanities and Social Science Curricula* 20 (1). https://www.asianstudies.org/publications/eaa/archives/the-philippines-an-overview-of-the-colonial-era/.

Holmes, J. and Brown, D.F. (1987). Teachers and students learning about compliments. *TESOL Quarterly* 21 (3): 523–546.

Hornsey, M.J., Greenaway, K.H., Bain, P.G. et al. (2018). Exploring cultural differences in the extent to which people perceive and desire control. *Personality and Social Psychology Bulletin* 45 (1): 81–92. https://journals.sagepub.com/doi/full/10.1177/0146167218780692.

Inglehart, R.F. (2018). *Cultural Evolution*. New York: Cambridge University Press.

Inglehart, R.F. and Welzel, C. (2005). *Modernization, Cultural Change, and Democracy: The Human Development Sequence*. New York: Cambridge University Press.

International Assignment Failure and Tracking Methods. (2021). Comment on the article "International assignment failure and tracking methods." The Forum for Expatriate Management (5 August). https://www.forum-expat-management.com/posts/11414-international-assignment-failure-and-tracking-methods#:%7E:text=Direct%20costs%20of%20a%20failed,with%20local%20business%20and%20government.

International Extension Curriculum. (n.d.). The Essence of Culture: A peek at Hispanics-Latinos Culture. Purdue University College of Agriculture. https://www.yumpu.com/en/document/read/11717026/the-essence-of-culture-a-peek-at-hispanics-college-of-agriculture-.

Jaiswal, S.K. and Choudhuri, R. (2017). A review of the relationship between parental involvement and students' academic performance. *The International Journal of Indian Psychology* 4 (3): 110–123.

Kasulis, K. (2017). South Korea's play culture is a dark symptom of overwork. Quartz (31 December). https://qz.com/1168746/south-koreas-play-culture-is-a-dark-symptom-of-overwork/.

Kemmelmeier, M. and Winter, D.G. (2000). What's in an American flag? National symbols prime cultural self-construals. Unpublished manuscript, University of Michigan.

Kim, Y.S., Leventhal, B.L., Koh, Y. et al. (2011). Prevalence of autism spectrum disorders in a total population sample. *American Journal of Psychiatry* 168 (9): 904–912.

Kowalski, R.B. and Fedina, C. (2011). Cyber bullying in ADHD and Asperger syndrome populations. *Research in Autism Spectrum Disorders* 5 (3): 1201–1208. https://www.sciencedirect.com/science/article/abs/pii/S1750946711000134?via%3Dihub.

Lectura Blog. (n.d.). How educators can reach out to Hispanic parents. Lectura Books. https://www.lecturabooks.com/educators-can-reach-hispanic-parents/.

Li, J. and Karakowsky, L. (2001). Do we see eye-to-eye? Implications of cultural differences for cross-cultural management research and practice. *The Journal of Psychology*, 135 (5): 501–517.

Lihua, Z. (2013). China's traditional cultural values and national identity. Carnegie Endowment for International Peace. https://carnegieendowment.org/2013/11/21/china-s-traditional-cultural-values-and-national-identity-pub-53613.

Mairian, C. and Sally, F. (1999). *Disability Discourse*. London: McGraw-Hill Education.

Mayes, S.D., Calhoun, S.L., Baweja, R., and Mahr, F. (2015). Maternal ratings of bullying and victimization: differences in frequencies between psychiatric diagnoses in a large sample of children. *Psychological Reports* 116 (3): 710–722.

Melendez, C. (2019). Dominican parenting across generations. Doctoral dissertation. University of Pennsylvania, https://www.proquest.com/docview/2388705978.

Moosa, S., Karabenick, S.A., and Adams, L. (n.d.). Teacher perceptions of Arab parent involvement in elementary schools. *The School Community Journal* 11 (2): 7–26). https://www.adi.org/journal/fw01/Moosa%20et%20al..pdf.

Naples, L.H. and Tuckwiller, E.D. (2021). Taking students on a strengths safari: a multidimensional pilot study of school-based wellbeing for young neurodiverse children. *International Journal of Environmental Research and Public Health* 18 (13): 6947. https://www.ncbi.nlm.nih.gov/pmc/articles/PMC8297144/.

OECD. (2006). *Personalising Education, Schooling for Tomorrow*. Paris: OECD Publishing. https://www.oecd-ilibrary.org/education/personalising-education_9789264036604-en.

Pittman, C.M. and Karle, E.M. (2019). *Rewire Your Anxious Brain: How to Use the Neuroscience of Fear to End Anxiety, Panic, and Worry* (Reprint ed.). Brattleboro, VT: Echo Point Books & Media.

Prera, A. (2020). Self-actualization. SimplyPsychology (4 September). https://www.simplypsychology.org/self-actualization.html.

Purdue Filipino. (n.d.). Basic Filipino history. https://purduefilipino.com/filipino-history#:~:text.

Rueda, R. and Stillman, J. (2012). The 21st century teacher: a cultural perspective. *Journal of Teacher Education* 63 (4): 245–253. https://www.researchgate.net/publication/258160286_The_21st_Century_Teacher_A_Cultural_Perspective.

Schaefer, R. (2006). *Sociology: A Brief Introduction*. New York: McGraw-Hill.

Shah, R.K. (2020). Complexities and contradictions in the implementation of learner centered teaching. *International Journal of Advanced Research in Education & Technology* 6 (4): 38–45.

Shavitt, S. and Zhang, J. (2004). Advertising and culture. In: *Encyclopedia of Applied Psychology* (ed. C.D. Spielberger). Amsterdam: Elsevier, 47–51. https://www.sciencedirect.com/science/article/pii/B0126574103000052.

Filipic Sterle, M., Fontaine, J.R.J., De Mol, J., and Verhofstadt, L.L. (2018). Expatriate family adjustment: an overview of empirical evidence on challenges and resources. *Frontiers in Psychology* 9: 1207. https://www.frontiersin.org/articles/10.3389/fpsyg.2018.01207/full.

Tesar, M. and Arndt, S. (2017). Cross-cultural complexities of educational policies. *Policy Futures in Education* 15 (6): 665–669.

Thomas. (2020). The Importance of cultural diversity in the workplace (17 March). https://www.thomas.co/resources/type/hr-blog/importance-cultural-diversity-workplace (accessed 16 February 2022).

UNESCO. (2014). Global citizenship education: preparing learners for the challenges of the 21st century. UNESDOC Digital Library. https://unesdoc.unesco.org/ark:/48223/pf0000227729 (accessed 16 February 2022).

Walden University. (n.d.). Why cultural diversity and awareness in the classroom is important. https://www.waldenu.edu/online-bachelors-programs/bs-in-elementary-education/resource/why-cultural-diversity-and-awareness-in-the-classroom-is-important (accessed 16 February 2022).

Weiner, B. and Grenier, M. (2020). Sensory balancing strategies for students with autism spectrum disorder. *Journal of Physical Education, Recreation & Dance* 91 (8), 21–28. https://www.tandfonline.com/doi/abs/10.1080/07303084.2020.1798308?journalCode=ujrd20.

Welzel, C. (2013). *Freedom Rising: Human Empowerment and the Quest for Emancipation.* Cambridge, UK: Cambridge University Press.

Witkin, H. and Berry, J.W. (1975). Psychological differentiation in cross-cultural perspective. *Journal of Cross-Cultural Psychology* (6): 4–87.

Williams, S.G. (2014). Communicating with Hispanic parents of young, school-age children. TRACE: Tennessee Research and Creative Exchange, University of Tennessee-Knoxville. https://trace.tennessee.edu/cgi/viewcontent.cgi?article=2756&context=utk_chanhonoproj.

Winch. G. (2013). Why some people hate receiving compliments: how self-esteem influences our capacity to receive praise. *Psychology Today* (27 August). https://www.psychologytoday.com/us/blog/the-squeaky-wheel/201308/why-some-people-hate-receiving-compliments.

World Values Survey. (n.d.). Impact and findings related to world culture. https://www.worldvaluessurvey.org/WVSContents.jsp?CMSID=Findings (accessed 16 February 2022).

Zwickert, L. (2017). How cultural norms in education differ around the world. EducationWeek (5 April). https://www.edweek.org/teaching-learning/opinion-how-cultural-norms-in-education-differ-around-the-world/2017/04 (accessed 13 March 2022).

CONCLUSION

This book has shared a wide array of research and many anecdotes on students and families coming from different cultural backgrounds that can reflect certain patterns of behavior, beliefs, and perceptions of the world. We hope the information will be useful for educators seeking to develop better relationships with their students, families, colleagues, and other stakeholders within their school community.

We wanted to close with a final anecdote from a high school student of ethnic Korean descent, "Ben."

During Ben's health class, the teacher, "Mr. K," was reviewing the effects of alcohol on adolescent and teenage brain development. As part of the teacher's dialogue with a highly multicultural class, he asked students from around the room about the drinking ages in their "home" countries.

He started with Jakub from Poland, who responded with, "18 years old, Mr. K."

Mr. K. continued, pointing to a boy from Ghana, "How about you, Abam?"

"18, as well."

"And Anna, how about Austria?"

"I think I'd say 16," Anna replied.

Mr. K went on and turned toward Ben. "Ben, what's the drinking age in Asia?"

Ben was about to respond, then paused as Mr. K.'s phrasing sank in.

Seconds went by that felt like minutes.

Ben recognized that the teacher knew he was ethnically Korean, but he was not asking about Korea but all of Asia. Though Ben was sure that Mr. K was aware that Asia was a continent, not a country, his skin color and facial appearance led him to make this slip.

As Ben knew Mr. K well and respected his friendliness and subject knowledge, he didn't feel deeply offended by the microaggression, but did feel a bit saddened by the reality of the world of categorizations and stereotypes. To others, he was Asian first and always would be. He wasn't Ben, the talented oboist who spoke three languages fluently (Korean wasn't one of them). Despite leaving Korea when he was two months old, he was still "stuck" in the eyes of even well-intentioned teachers like Mr. K.

Mr. K coughed gently, bringing Ben out of this series of realizations. At that moment, Ben knew exactly how to respond.

"I wouldn't know, Mr. K, I'm from Argentina."

The point of this story, and, indeed, the message of this book, is that our understanding of cultural backgrounds should only, and in fact can only, serve as general advice for possible ways to interact more successfully.

Even the most well-intentioned and well-prepared educator will make a faulty assumption, rush to judgment, or say the wrong thing. Attempting to understand and appreciate the core beliefs and values that may alter the perceptions and communications is a noble endeavor, but also one with an inherent possibility of error, which many parents will understand.

We all wish to serve students and families as best we can, which means understanding there will always be exceptions—and sometimes can become the new norm—as individual experiences are shaped by innate traits, socioeconomic class, gender, age, family ties, travel, relocations, and more.

This is what's most exciting about attempts to better interact with other cultures—it requires celebrating what makes us educators: the ability to change, adapt, and embrace the beauty of the world and the people who live in it together with us.

INDEX

Page numbers followed by *f* refer to figures.